Edited by Fucina Srl, Via Ennio 8, 20137 Milan, Italy
Tel. 02.55189946 Fax 02.55181329
E-mail: info@fucinaeditore.it
Internet: www.fucinaeditore.it

All the photos in this book are from Giacomo Agostini's personal collection.
Where the author's name is not indicated the editor shall be
at the disposal of any entitled parties.

ISBN 88-88269-12-6

Giacomo Agostini   Luca Delli Carri

Fifteen Times

Fucina

Contents

Fangio was one of those practical people
who always looked skyward before going out,
just to see if an umbrella is needed.
That's how he got to his present age
without even a scratch on his bodywork
or a dent in his bumper.
He lived at a speed in which luck
was as important as skill.
He raced cheek by jowl with death
and gazed upon it in horror.
And in the end the he retired quietly,
without fuss.
OSVALDO SORIANO

Preface

What's the point in presenting a champion only in terms of what he has achieved? What is the point in imagining a champion to be as machine-like as his motorcycle, racing car or javelin? What is the point is thinking of him in terms of pure performance, as no more than a man engaged in a struggle for supremacy and, all said and done, survival?

In short, there is *no* point. A champion is a man, and only has meaning when presented as such, together with his merits and defects, his quirks and habits *and* his moments of sporting glory. Only then – just as we might learn how a politician comes to power by looking into his life and analysing its day-by-day details – can we hope to comprehend how a rider became a champion.

Giacomo Agostini's story is a remarkable one. In the entire history of motorcycling, no-one has won more than him. He dominated the World Motorcycling Championship for a stunning ten years (1966-1975), doing so in both the 350 and 500 cc categories. He was what every racer aspired to be, yet was also their chief obstacle - the rocky cliff between the shipwrecked sailor and the salvation of landfall. Agostini was simply the best and the others just had to be content with second place. That was how it was to the end, right up to the very last races of his career; only after a seemingly endless period of domination - a period that would, today, be unimaginable - would he be beaten by a younger generation of riders.

There was, however, much more to Giacomo Agostini than this: he personified the star, the successful sportsman, the unreachable, the Latin lover. Few racing car drivers or motorcycle riders have enjoyed so much off-track popularity. Yet above all, more than any other champion, he was just what the sixties and his country had been waiting for: handsome, Mediterranean temperament, the perfect dark-haired fine-featured Italian. It was a mix that would make him an idol.

His secret? Perhaps it was this: if you meet his gaze, even today, you will see the kindness of a refined man mixed with the hunger of an animal observing its prey. The contrast between these two personas sparked the genesis of an unequalled champion. He may not have had more talent than his rivals (see Hailwood, Saarinen, Roberts), but he was endowed with an iron willpower that crushed everyone and more than one rider lost his life trying to keep up with him. When he hit the track, he was, in his own mind, the undisputed leader and the others the also-rans who could do no more than bear the harsh truth of Agostini's superiority.

Yet a champion cannot be explained just by catching the glint in his eye. You have to get him to talk and tell. Then you need to see him in action, study his lifestyle, peek at the details. Only then can you hope to gain the insight that will lead you to the man behind the mask. And this in-depth research, rather than belittling the champion, actually feeds the legend. Because a clear comprehension of what made him the king of his sport does not, in fact draw him any nearer to us: if anything, it makes him seem even more distant, unreal, unique and exceptional. Snippets from his life, his shortcomings and quirks reveal how he managed to reach the mountaintop before anyone else and how he prevented anyone else from rising up to take his place for years.

This book intends to go beyond Giacomo Agostini the man and rider. It aims, once and for all, to destroy the myth of the champion-by-chance, just a cocktail of genius and wildness. Real champions are not "accountants" of speed, as was said of Niki Lauda, but rather, "engineers" of speed. They are precise to the point of being pedantic, even tedious, incessant in their requests. Requests that, seen close up, are always small: because the winning rider is the one with the right mix of essential factors: a finely-tuned bike, an awareness that everything possible has been done, close support, and a sharp-edged hunger for victory that, in top competitors, is never assuaged. Simple things that transform a talented rider into a great champion. The public figure – and Agostini was certainly that – was quite a different matter. It was as if there were two people co-habiting in the same body: the one who gets on his motorcycle and races, and the one who gets off and waves to the photographers. Every great champion gives this impression: from Agostini to Valentino Rossi, from motorcycle riders to racing car drivers, whatever the epoch.

Above all then, what the details behind the Agostini story show us is his meticulousness, determination and single-mindedness. Behind the image of the successful rider surrounded by women, who wins effortlessly thanks to pure talent, lies a little man who is a pain in the neck to his mechanics, his technicians, the team managers and the motorcycle, tyre and accessory suppliers: a man who constantly demands technical solutions designed for him and him alone.

So it was with Agostini: an outstanding performer on the motorcycle and an outstanding worker *for* the motorcycle. After retirement he found further success with his own team, in public relations, in the promotion of his own persona. Something of a prisoner of his own popularity, yes, but it has been so with many sporting heroes. They never quite manage to divest themselves of their "winning" ways. And is there anything wrong in that? The world loved them for what they were, and despite the years they continue to give off that aura of victory. All we can do is applaud them and envy their seemingly perfect, unblemished lives.

Tape n° 1
The stuff of champions

Carlo Zerbi, nicknamed Nao because he always said no and pronounced it "nao", sipped his coffee and popped a biscuit into his mouth. He'd been having that same coffee-and-biscuits breakfast every morning for the past nine years, ever since he went to live on his own. As usual, he was just staring into space. Not for any particular reason, mind you: it was just that, apart from the kitchen wall, there was nothing else to look at. It had never crossed his mind to hang up a poster or a photo, let alone a painting, and his house was accordingly bare. There wasn't even a pinup calendar. And this was perfectly in keeping with the sort of person he was: Nao had no desires, no curiosity and no whims. He liked to talk, but just for the sake of a chat, not to understand others. He liked staying out until late but not so late as to be groggy the next morning. He liked the bachelor's life: eating at his favourite haunts, shooting the breeze with prostitutes and pimps and feeling the nightlife flow around him without it in any way affecting him. And he loved his work. He was a journalist who wrote about cars. He was pretty good, let's say normal. Most of all he did editorial work: he was destined to become one of those super-sedentary types, who, from their black plastic swivel chairs upholstered in red, know and judge the entire world, especially the other journalists and freelancers who send in their pieces so that Nao and his colleagues can set them straight and make them pageworthy. Without the tweaking of the super-sedentary editors, believed Nao, those writings would remain both useless and unread.

In short, his life was squarer than a Rubik's cube. It had been years since he'd been able to remember a dream; if asked he'd probably have said that he'd never dreamt a night in his life. He didn't even have the usual daydreams such as having a girlfriend or family. The following year he'd pay off the mortgage on the flat he'd bought in an outlying district. It was just a cramped two-roomed affair, but it would be *his*. Home ownership gave him pleasure, a sense of being above-average, or at least above the average of the people he came into contact with - whether they were journalists like himself or wayward night-lifers, because other types Nao knew not. And in both cases it didn't take much to feel a bit different or a bit better, because for the most part they had no ambitions, dreams or desires either. People like him who had just let themselves go a bit more. Nao, instead, in his own peculiar way, kept a grip on himself: he wanted to be good super-sedentary so as to be able to earn a little money and second a few whims, to gain a better position and perhaps preside over the lower echelons. He knew it was just a question of time: all he had to do was never give up, always be ready and willing, kind and respectful towards the people who counted. His limited talent was almost an irrelevance, because his job didn't require talent. Instead, it demanded obstinacy, attention, a pinch of contempt for those who sent in the articles and needed to acknowledge the necessity of Nao's corrective hand in much the same way as a child accepts his father's guidance.

Behind the wheel, he immediately got stuck in traffic. Although he often wrote about some of the finest, most expensive cars in the world, his own automobile was a plain Citroen runabout.

He took a shortcut and started to sidestep the river of cars flooding into the city, striving, just like his, to get to their owners' place of work. He knew all the shortcuts between his home and the publisher's and back, and this was another thing that made him feel smart and on the ball.

When driving, he switched off mentally. He drove, full stop. In fact, he rarely thought at all: he just thought of what he had to do when he had to do it. Just like a machine that comes on only when needed. Otherwise, his life consisted of passing away the hours and days in as pleasant and stress-free a way as possible. And as he was extremely self-centred, he was good at it.

However, because he never thought outside office hours, he did not, that morning, think this was the day in which he would start work on the biography of Giacomo Agostini, or 'the Winner' as Nao had taken to calling him. He knew he would, after work, go home and switch on his home computer and get started on it, yet he had not thought about what he'd write or even wanted to write. He would, quite simply, get cracking. He's gather up the tapes he'd made during their meetings, put them in the player and start listening. He'd take notes from the most interesting excerpts and would later decide how to work then into the text and in what order. He had no idea whether he'd write a book that started with the Agostini's birth and ended with his retirement from racing or whether he'd have a series of subject-related chapters: the motorcycles, the races, the women, the cars and so on. Yet, all told, not knowing what he would do didn't scare him. After all, he hadn't thought about it, not even for five minutes. He'd consider it as the day went on, during office hours. He knew it wasn't going to be easy as the Winner wanted a "different" kind of book, something deeper than the usual end-of-sportsman's-career biography. When they had met for the first time, Agostini had promised to tell him everything – *everything* – about his life: the behind-the-scenes goings-on, unprecedented revelations. Instead, he'd ended up saying all the usual things that sportsmen say: that, all said and done, their lives were passionately dedicated to their sport and all the rest was just a sideshow.

Nao had had this impression confirmed twice. First by a TV special on Agostini, in which he'd given the low-down on his career and life in exactly the same way as he had with Nao. Secondly, he'd remembered a book by Richard Ford he'd read a year before, the main protagonist of which was a sports journalist. He'd dug the book out and, on flicking through it, had luckily come across the bit he was interested in (and so avoided having to read the whole thing again). It went: "As regards athletes, I have just one thing to say: you can get to know them all too well, to the point of getting fed up with them, as happens with everyone. If you study them too closely they all look alike: predictable and factual. That's why I sometimes say less than I know: I reckon, for what it's worth, that youngsters in my line of work make the mistake of interviewing too deeply".

Nao, at this point, understandably asked himself what he should do, whether there was any chance of this project amounting to anything and, above all, whether he really should dig deep, and write about absolutely everything he could find out about the Winner – even if it meant going against the Winner's own wishes. After all, he probably just wanted a nice, well-written hagiography, not exactly the usual retired sportsman's story but something only *ever so slightly* less foregone, and his interest in the content was such that he wouldn't even read it, but would have it read by his secretary (he'd even said so to Nao; the Winner was interested in the book as a finished product, something to trade with, a business card, a done deal).

Since, however, none of these questions had found an immediate answer, Nao had thought about it no more and had not even thought about what he wanted to do. All he'd done was to write the book's starting date on his calendar, and that day was now upon him: that evening he would start to deal with the Winner's life story.

After driving to the Egyptian pizzeria with the imitation marble walls, eating his pizza in solitude, downing a glass of lager and eavesdropping on the conversation (which wasn't very juicy, unfortunately)at the neighbouring table, Nao went home and gave the tour of his usual haunts a miss. He changed into his tracksuit and the electric-blue slippers he'd stolen from a luxury hotel in Munich (he always did that: he nicked slippers, bars of soap, shampoo, needle and thread, as, after all, they were consumables placed at the customer's disposal. However, he only took the good, refined-looking stuff; at home he had boxes of it). He sat at his computer and switched it on, then picked up the tape recorder and the first tape. There were seven of them: seven tapes made at the Winner's home, a stunning villa above Bergamo that Agostini had built from the proceeds of his first racing wins. It was a single-story affair, with a large basement containing a gym and Agostini's personal office, cloakroom and garage. Nothing in the garage reminded the visitor of the Winner's twenty years of racetrack success, except the fairing of one of his spent motorcycles, casually cast aside like any other worn out object. Upstairs in the living quarters were his cups and photos. There was also a table on which he'd gathered together all the key photos from his life, including those of his family: Nao had gazed on this table with pleasure, as it had given him a measure of the satisfaction, wealth and serenity felt by a man who has had everything from life.

It was an early 1970s villa, with columns and a well-kept lawn. The Winner was a perfectionist, always had been, and this had been a key factor in his success. His attention to detail, his manic organisational precision, his need for efficiency, was reflected in the house. The portico gutter pipes ended with a lightweight chain so that the rainwater would drain off the roof at exactly the desired point only. After all, control of the situation is one of the necessary characteristics of a champion, in sport or in life. And Nao, in his own way, always had control of the situation. Of course, his life was vastly different from the Winner's. It was, to be honest, a pretty squalid life, yet within that squalor Nao had set himself rules and stuck by them so as to make sure that everything went as planned. And the great thing was that the strategy worked: things really went the way he wanted them to. Little things, of no importance to others, but things that made him feel on-top and tough, capable of dominating things.

In the Winner's villa, the living area showed evident care in the choice of materials: leather sofas, plasma TV, a long antique dining table. Evidence of Agostini's success was everywhere: the top shelf stashed with trophies, then the helmets, then the race photos. Everything was as neat and ordered as can be. Yet it wasn't just a question of exhibiting trophies: more importantly, everything was exactly where the Winner wanted it to be.

Beyond the French windows lay the garden. A restless Cocker Spaniel stuck its wet nose up against the glass, then scuttled off, wagging its tail, when Agostini had chased it off with a shout. A little further away lay the swimming pool: a luxury even today, never mind in the seventies.

Before playing back the tape, Nao picked up one of the biographies that had already been written about the Winner. He peered at the cover photo, as if looking for inspiration.

Yes, there he was: Giacomo Agostini, fifteen times world champion, the rider who has clocked up more victories than anyone else in the entire history of motorcycling. "I'm still the best, until anyone beats that record", he'd once said to Nao, with an air of satisfaction and feisty competitiveness clearly aimed at today's riders.

Because, although he'd hung up his helmet over a quarter of a century ago, he was still a racer at heart. He was a competitor, a *winner*. And he'd never given up the role of champion, a role he'd started playing at the age of twenty and still played. A role he would probably never relinquish. Because real winners, like him, are *always* winners. They are not the champions who last a season or two, nor the eternal runners-up adored by the fans but who fail to deliver the killer blow. Real winners *keep on* winning, dominating entire eras, maintaining their authoritativeness and the hard-won air of invincibility even when they retire.

Giacomo Agostini, in fact, belonged to that tiny circle of ex-racers who were sought-after guest stars. Like Jackie Stewart and Stirling Moss, he could command a healthy cachet: whether it was the presentation of a new motorcycle or a race commemoration, he got paid for it. And this fact, exceptional in the racing world, was not just because he had won more than anyone else: it was because he was a *winner*.

Nao pressed "Play"…

NAO What is celebrity?

GIACOMO Some say that fame can drive you barmy, with all those people wanting your autograph. I actually think it's rather splendid, something to be proud of because it means you've made something of your life and people acknowledge you for it. Fame opens many doors. Some do take advantage of you, of course because they fail to understand that you're just like anyone else, but there's no denying fame's a huge help. At the height of my career, whenever I left my small hometown of Lovere to dine out in Milan or Brescia, there was always a table for me. There was *always* room for Agostini - at the bar, in the restaurant or anywhere else. It was all because I was famous. Many dislike all this: to them I say, "Work as pharmacist, or sit behind a desk for thirty years and then tell me what you think". When I was team manager, there were riders who didn't want people in the paddocks as they felt irritated by them. "Look", I'd tell them, "if you weren't a motorcycle racer you'd be a factory worker and you'd be earning a factory worker's wage, so if you're here earning millions it's thanks to those people that come to see you, that inconvenience you with their demands for an autograph". Instead they expect the world to leave them alone. Even Eddie Lawson found the attention bothersome. I told him the truth: if we want to be protagonists, if we want to earn well, if we want to do this job which is so in the public eye, then we have to accept the public's presence. If you want to be left alone, get a job at the steelworks. It's thanks to those people that you become someone, that you earn your money. If no-one comes to watch us race, if there's no enthusiasm, it's like writing a book no-one will ever read.

NAO How do you ride the tiger of celebrity, from both a personal and economic standpoint?

GIACOMO You need to be extremely careful, because fame cuts both ways: it lets you meet so many people, but it also draws you out of your entourage, your habits. You meet people from all over the world. They might or might not be honest and when you can't tell the difference trouble is on its way. I'll never forget the words of Gino Bartali (famed Italian cyclist and Tour de France winner), who I met on several occasions. Like many at that time, he called me Mino. He always used to say: "Mino, I want you to know that I earned a fortune as a cyclist - today we'd be talking about millions. Yet little or nothing remains of it; a garage in Florence, one or two apartments... Because during my career I met a lot of people who suggested investments to make me even richer, and most of them were rip-offs. Even when I started making the Bartali bicycles I got ripped off, because when you're focussed on your sport, your career, you don't have the time or the desire to think about anything else, so you delegate. And, since the world is full of scoundrels...". This is the downside of fame: you can end up trusting someone who goes on to ruin you. You've risked your life, raced for years on end, worked hard and made endless sacrifices and you end up with nothing because some conman or freebooter has taken your earnings and invested them into oblivion. You need to be alert, because things can either keep on getting better - or things can go down the drain.

NAO Did any other racers ever speak to you about failing to manage their earnings properly?

GIACOMO Without naming names, I have to say yes, there were lots of them. It's important not to get greedy. You might be doing well and get the urge to do more, boost the earnings. Take it easy, do one thing at a time I say: if you're earning reasonably and are committed then making your money work for you is all well and fine. But do it without greed, without taking on too many things at a time. It's the wisest way because a sport like mine consumes nearly all your time and mental energy. Back then, falling off was out of the question. Falling meant dying as the circuits were downright dangerous: where the tarmac finished the guardrail, the trees and the walls began: there was no safety margin. I remember, despite the eagerness to race, that we were also worried and afraid: don't think we weren't. While the passion can make you forget it for a while, the fear is always there. We often came back from a Grand Prix with one friend or companion less. Today, thank goodness, huge steps have been made on the safety side; thanks to us, and in part thanks to strikes that I led myself. I've always hated the word "strike", but for safety's sake there were some races that I just had to pull out of. For example, there was once snow on the ground on pre-race day and a rider fell during practice; he died, I think, and I said there was no way I was going to ride on ice or near-ice. It was deplorable. Unfortunately, though, many riders were all too willing to be on the starting grid, because they got 200 thousand liras just for participating and they needed that money to fund the transfer to the following week's venue. These riders – from Australia, some Italians, some Brits – turned up in their caravans and got 150-200 thousand liras per race, and if they refused to ride they had no money to move on to the next event. These guys wanted to race at any cost, while some of the others, myself included, wanted to see some change. One reason for this was a terrible experience I'd had – one I still think of today. I was at the Vallelunga track in Rome. We'd hired out the circuit to test the MV. The whole track was reserved for us and us alone. This kid, about eighteen years old, comes up and asks me: "Agostini, can I try out my 125?". So I say "Sure, you clock up a few laps too". I'd felt sorry for him, you see: there we were with the whole track to ourselves and him with squat. However, soon after he got going he fell at a bend, then stood up: both his arms had been amputated. It was Lazzarini, the brother of Eugenio Lazzarini, who went on to be World Champion. Imagine that boy's sheer sadness, losing his arms like that... I'd given him permission to ride and when he'd picked himself up off the ground he had no arms... If it had happened on a modern track without guardrails, he'd have been fine. I struggled to bring an end to such things. For example, I was hated because, after Parlotti[1] died, I packed in the Tourist Trophy. The evening before he'd asked me to drive him round the course. He said "Seeing as you know the route better than me, take me round in the car". Dinner's served early in Britain and at that time of year it's light until ten or ten-thirty, so we started off at seven in the evening. His 125 race was scheduled for 9.30 in the morning, and I was due to start in the 500 at 11.30. He knew the course, but not as well as I did, because I'd been racing there for some years by then. The next day, I was in the pits getting ready for the start, my leathers already on, when I noticed the look on the mechanics' faces: I instantly knew that Parlotti, who had been leading, had fallen and was dead. By then it was almost 11.30 and there was no backing out. But imagine how I felt: just the evening before I'd taken him for a spin in the car and in the morning he was gone – all because of a fall. Another rider had died two days earlier. Remember, two, tree or four riders died at every TT. So I said "That's it, I'm through with the TT. If we fall because of an error or a mechanical fault, a broken chain, a burst tyre or a patch of oil, then

NOTE:[1] Gilberto Parlotti (1940, 4 GP wins in 125) died at the TT race in' 72 on a Morbidelli 125.

you've got to give us the chance to live. It's not on, this business of falling and inevitably dying". Yet the Brits thought we had to be all heroic and risk big, because that was our job – that we had to demonstrate we were prepared to look death in the eye. I struggled for a long time with the British: I've always said the Tourist Trophy is one of the most beautiful circuits in the world, a rider's circuit, and that if you can win the TT you're a true champion, because the track has everything: the uphill, the downhill, the jumps, the downhill bends, the bridges, the flyover, the counter-sloping bend... it has it all. But then there's the fog and the rain, and in the space of a lap you can run into fog, rain and wind at different points. If you fell you were a goner. To me this was wrong. I struggled against the Brits until we succeeded in getting the TT removed from the World Championship calendar. I got support from Barry Sheene and Phil Read too, because they realised they were losing a friend every year and we just couldn't go on like that. I'm proud I made that stand, just as I did with other dangerous circuits, such as the one in Czechoslovakia, where there was no escape if you came off. I did once fall at the TT, luckily on a slow uphill section: it had rained the day before and water was still seeping from the tarmac. Hailwood, in front of me, had fallen because he'd also hit the seepage. At TT races we were started off at ten-second intervals, and I'd left 10 seconds after him; I hit the same patch of water, no more than 10 cm wide, and I fell at exactly the same point. He got up, kicked the bent footrest back into place and took off but my bike was damaged and I was forced to withdraw.

NAO How did you feel when you saw Parlotti's mechanics and found out about his fall?

GIACOMO I asked my own mechanics what had happened and they told me that Parlotti had fallen. I could see the sadness in their faces and the tears welling up in their eyes, and I realized he was gone, because I knew that if you fell there you'd had it. Only Hailwood and I survived, but if we'd fallen at a different point... On the Isle of Man you slammed into a wall at 200 kph: what good do you think a crash helmet and leathers are going to do you at that speed?

NAO Before starting your own race, did you remove any thought of the accident and Parlotti's death?

GIACOMO Of course. I said to myself: "What can I do? This is my job, I'm here, it's terribly sad – but I have to race". So I did. I knew there was nothing I could do to get out of it: the organisation was under way, we knew it was dangerous, we knew that we might die - but we just had to race. It's the day after that it hits you, just as the tragic deaths of Pasolini and Saarinen at Monza[1] did. That Sunday I took part in the 500 race, immediately after theirs. Yet on the Monday I was here, sat right here at home, and I sobbed because I realised it could happen to anyone and it's nobody's fault if you finish against the guardrail or if you manage to leap from the skidding bike only to be killed by the one coming up behind you. It could have happened to me as much as anyone else. It's like when you hear about an airline disaster and you say "It's terrible, but it won't happen to me". You have to say that to give you the strength to go on, otherwise you wouldn't get on any more planes and I wouldn't have got on any more motorcycles. It's the defence mechanism that lets you keep going.

NAO Tell me more about the race tracks.

GIACOMO When I started racing, the race tracks were what they were. What was I supposed to do? I couldn't ask them to change them. However, once I started to understand that deaths could be prevented then I did what I could. I didn't get much support, because they used to say to me "Sure, for you it's easy. You travel first class, turn up in your Porsche and have a truck with eight mechanics to take care of you...". They just didn't understand that when there was an accident, when your life was on the line, that we were all equal, that my life was as fragile as theirs.

NAO Who were they?

GIACOMO A group that toured the circuits, made up of Aussies, Kiwis, South Africans... They were paid by the race and certainly weren't winners. They had private motorcycles, paid for out of their own pockets. They did the arithmetic and said "I do fifteen grand prix races, earn 300 thousand liras per Grand Prix, which gives me four million liras a year and that'll do me". They were Jack Horn, Tom Phillis, Tommy Robb, Jim Redman, Jack Findlay, some of whom went on to become official riders and World Champions. When it was winter here they went home where it was summer and did the race season there. They'd turn up with their wives, some already had kids. The wife was often a mechanic, and I remember the

NOTE:[1] Jarno Saarinen (Finland 1945) won the World 250 Championship in '72 on a Yamaha and 15 GPs in 250, 350 and 500 between '71 and '73. Renzo Pasolini (Rimini 1938) won six GPs in 250 between '69 and '72. They died in the same accident at Monza, on 20th May 1973.

kids used to hang out in the pits and the caravans all day long, playing and getting grubby... I always knew I'd never be able to race with a family in tow, or see my kids just before the start of a race, because at the time there were a lot of deaths in motorcycling and we thought about it all the time. Three years later, when I was working as a Grand Prix commentator for RAI (the Italian state television), there were fifty-three falls at the Sachsenring from Friday to Sunday. Jim Redman was there with us and I said to him "In my day fifty-three falls would have meant at least three deaths". In fact, we never had anywhere near that number of falls: we simply couldn't afford to, as fifty-three would have meant three of four corpses at least. So you see, it was the circuits that were the problem. And the riders didn't have adequate protection either: Dainese has since done much to make the suits safer, just as Nolan has the helmets, and the race tracks finally have a run-off so that when you fall you just slide. A lot of people ask me what happens when you fall at 250 kph. That depends. Because if you fall at 250 kph as you're leaning right into the bend and the bike skids away from you the slide is inconsequential – very spectacular, but banal. It's when you hit or slide into a solid object that you get hurt. How much of your body do you think is going to be left intact when you hit a tree, a wall, or a guardrail at 250 kph? The guardrail could slice you to pieces... The big struggle was against Formula 1, because the racing car teams wanted the tracks to be lined with guardrails, just like those radio-controlled car tracks, to keep the cars on the asphalt. Since they had more clout we just had to put up with their choices. Then they realised two things: first, that Formula 1 cars had lateral fuel tanks that caught fire when they scraped against the guardrail and, secondly, that every time they made some small error and hit the guardrail the car got damaged. Today they just spin off onto the grass and rejoin the race. The insurance companies stopped covering the cars because even a minor skid would smash up the ailerons and that was expensive damage. Just some silly mistake and – bang! – you had serious problems. If it happens now you roll out onto the grass, turn round, come back and get going again. Luckily for us, people began to grasp this and the Formula 1 teams also started saying "Maybe it's better to remove the guardrails and make room for run-offs". It made a huge difference to us motorcycle riders, I can tell you, but in the beginning it was hard going because they saw the track as something that had to contain the car and not let it escape.

NAO Did the riders ever discuss death amongst themselves?

GIACOMO Well, it wasn't spoken of the way you and I are doing now. However, when I went off racing and kissed my mother goodbye I knew I might never see her again. I knew it, but my love and passion for motorcycling was absolute and I accepted the risks that came with it. It was a career you embarked on, especially in those days, out of a mad love affair with motorbikes. I've wanted to race motorcycles since I was a very young child. It was practically a craving: some people tried their luck at football, then, disappointed, tried their luck at motorcycling. Not me. Right from the start I said "I want to race motorcycles". I didn't give a damn about anything else.

NAO So the rider thinks that accidents can happen – but never to him?

GIACOMO Sure, an accident might happen, but I'm just so lucky, or Jesus is with me, and so I'm gonna be all right. That's how you build up your courage: that's how I reckon most people do.

NAO So you're a rider, you know you could get killed or hurt, but it's as if this reality doesn't exist, as if it were something outside you, that has nothing to do with you.

GIACOMO Yes, the risk is there, but you tell yourself: "It isn't going to happen to me. I'm lucky, a born survivor". That's how it's done, there's no alternative is there? Before the start of a race we were tenser than riders are today, because in addition to the concentration, the pressure and the will to win, we had more risks to contend with. There are still plenty of falls, but when you race and see it happen time after time without consequence, it bolsters your courage. In fact, there are more and more falls now: not because the riders are any less skilled or because they push the envelope more, it's just that they know a fall is not, in itself, as serious a thing as it was in my day. Facts and statistics bear me out on this: the number of falls today has more than doubled.

NAO Were there riders who never thought about the accidents, who really didn't give a damn about anything?

GIACOMO Us Italians were perhaps a bit heartier, more sensitive, perhaps a bit more attached to life - or perhaps just a bit less arrogant than some of the foreigners who liked to think of themselves (and the world to think of them) as being hard, like the ones who strolled about with their leathers unzipped to show off their pecs. There are people who think like that, after all. For example, my brother was a boxer, and if you were to clash with him and pull out a knife and say something like "Watch it, or I'll stick you good", he would coolly say "Try it". Not me. Some people are just different, have more spirit perhaps. Maybe some people do say "Yeah, dying's all right. When? Tomorrow? Good a time as any". I've heard plenty of talk like that, but I couldn't honestly say whether it was sincere or just bravado.

NAO Yet for you it was different: you were fully aware of everything.

GIACOMO I knew the risks. Yet I still wanted a career in motorcycling: and, risking everything that had to be risked, that's what I got.

Nao stopped the tape and looked at his watch. It was five past midnight.

He got up, strolled into the kitchen, opened the fridge and took a bottle of German beer. He returned to the table, took his first sip and relished the moment in which the icily refreshing liquid slid down his throat.

Yes, he thought, he had liked the 'Winner'. He was confident, highly motivated. He spoke quickly, but never hurried his words. It was simply as if he had no time to waste and therefore allotted each word just enough time to get out of his mouth in a comprehensible fashion.

The first time they'd met was for an interview. He hadn't liked him then: Agostini had come across as disagreeable, one of those people who only does something if he perceives some profit in it. All told, that was how the Winner was. But wasn't it so for everyone? Nao, after all, only did things if there was something in it for him. Anyone with a spark of ambition does only what is "useful". And to win, you have to be like that.

During that first interview, in a bar along a traffic-clogged avenue in Bergamo, the Winner had answered the questions in a rush, not exactly giving one-word answers but coming close, as if the interview were a hindrance to be dealt with as fast as possible. Nevertheless, he'd been polite and had completed the interview: and it was a good one too, because Agostini had come across as smart and sincere and Nao's questions had been original and the Winner had liked them too: a seasoned pub conversationalist, Nao knew how to get people talking.

Yet that initial interview had left him with the lasting image of a person who could be deadly. Deadly, yes, that was the word. A man with an iron will who had goals and did anything to achieve them. A man who had not stopped in front of anything and never would.

Nao stood up and fetched the interview, which had later been published in a book. He sought out the passage he was interested in: the death of Angelo Bergamonti, the Winner's team-mate, at Riccione in '71.

He read: "It was a tragedy. I was out in front right from the start and had built up a lead of seven or eight seconds. The rain had made the track as treacherous as ice. Seeing as I had a sizeable advantage I slowed a little. But instead of doing the same, he pushed it to catch me up. He took a second or two, maybe three, from me and closed the gap to five seconds. So I turned up the throttle again. I thought "It's lethal out here, I've shown him he can't keep up, so why's he pushing it?'. So I started doing laps at the speed I'd started at. Then, regrettably, he fell. He wanted to beat me, but when he saw he was losing a second and a half per lap he should have realised it was hopeless. If you ease up, I ease up so we can both finish the race safe and sound. It was fate: his wheels slid out from under him, but it could just as easily have happened to me".

These words gave Nao the shivers, just as they did when he first heard them, and Nao did not think of himself as being easily upset. The Winner really had been a deadly rider, and he was still, most likely, a deadly man today.

NAO Sunday was race day. How do you recall those days?

GIACOMO The Sunday was the last day of all the tension and stress that had started building up on the Friday. You'd get up soaked in apprehension, waking up early because of the anxiety. If it was a hard or an important race your stomach would be churning. Your heart rate went up too. Personally, I used to sleep all right, but as soon as I was awake I said: "Blast it, today I've got to race". I've *got to*, I used to say to myself: but the truth was that I *wanted* to. If the race was scheduled for 2 pm then I'd have breakfast at around nine or nine-thirty; yet it was hard getting the food down. I couldn't swallow and some things I couldn't eat at all. I practically had to force it down, at the cost of effort. Usually, I wolf my food down but on Sunday mornings I'd eat listlessly and it would sometimes take me half an hour to finish that breakfast. On talking with the great cyclist Gimondi I discovered that he had steak for breakfast; of course, being a cyclist, he needed the energy. Yet cyclists didn't put their lives on the line, while we did, another factor that probably had a lot to do with my lack of appetite. The only things I could get down were a boiled egg or a bit of ham. Pasta wasn't popular back then as everyone thought it bloated you so I'd try some plain rice with a little olive oil. Absolutely no appetite, of course, but I knew I had to eat, because the oomph would have to be there later on. Yes, breakfast was quite a struggle! Then I'd head for the race track. I'd feel fresh and strong; I'd greet all the others, but afterwards I had no idea who I'd waved or smiled at. Once on the track the people would crush in and that was when it got overwhelming because friends and fans would all swarm around at once. I mean, absolutely everyone would be there: fans, friends, people from the host town. It's not like you can plan it, not like when you say "Today I'll meet three people, tomorrow I'll go to Como and meet some others". No. They *all* wanted to say hello. I found it stressful, as did all the other riders. Look how Valentino Rossi hides away - and who can blame him: it's a time when you don't want to see anyone because you're so tense. You just don't feel like chit-chat. My strength lay in being able to keep up a smile, but I didn't even know who I was talking to unless it was a close relative or friend. My mind was elsewhere – in the race, on the bike. I'd be thinking "I'll press on, accelerate, I'll win... Will the bike break down or not? If I win this one I'll get so many points, if I win that one instead...". The public loved me – and I loved them too; because when you're there on the starting grid all those people really psyche you up. When I saw the public cheering I thought "Don't let them down. Show them what you're made of". Yet just before the race, when I was out there on the grid, with only three minutes to go, if someone came up to me and asked for an autograph I'd say neither yes nor no, because I didn't have the strength to do either. The strength also left me when I had to push the bike – or that's how it seemed anyway. I'd be so exhausted by the tension that I'd ask myself "Will I be able to push the bike?". Then when the flag dropped the strength would flood back into me – and how! I guess it was just a natural gift.

NAO What did you do in the hours leading up to the start?

GIACOMO It would take me about half an hour to get my kit on and it had to be done just right. I'd gather my stuff together, check the socks, turn them inside out, put them on, take them off, then put them back on again – the right one first. Then on would go the yellow T-shirt, a constant companion; after I'd check I was buttoned up properly... I liked to be able to dress calmly, as it was a good way of passing the time and lessening the concentration and stress. I also had a big advantage: I managed to sleep before the start. Not for long, just enough to re-energise and end the tension. I'd sleep ten minutes, fifteen at most, but I'd be totally unconscious and when I woke up I felt much stronger than I had done a quarter of an hour previously.

NAO When did you sleep?

GIACOMO Half an hour before the start. I'd have a kip in the team van, perhaps kitted up and race-ready, or sometimes before getting ready when the tension was draining me. I'd just say "What's the hurry? Let's just have forty winks". I probably slept to blot out the tension. Remember, I had a lot of responsibility weighing on me: as might be expected, whenever I participated in races where I knew I didn't have a chance, I was always more relaxed. The pressure came from everyone *expecting* me to win and so I felt responsible. For example, MV just *had* to win, as did Morini and Yamaha. There was always this responsibility towards a whole group of people, all waiting for me to give them victory. Of course, there was plenty to be happy about too: I had a great motorcycle, an outstanding team – but the anxiety was never far off. Although I pretended and always smiled, I felt obliged to produce a result and so I was always tense prior to the start. I'd always go onto the track at the last possible moment, not because I was a snob or so that someone could say "Here comes the superstar". No. It was because I felt worse on the track: I wanted to stay hidden to the last second. Instead there was all this gossip that Agostini wanted to be the leading light who always arrived at the last moment to maintain the interest in him.

Images from a film clip he'd seen popped into Nao's mind. In it the Winner was waiting on the starting grid with the other riders. He was the only one smiling and joking. There was Jarno Saarinen, with the sad face of a man with pure talent who hasn't yet tasted success. There was Renzo Pasolini, always a bit serious, always rather intense, always a bit unhappy with himself. Agostini – the Winner – was, instead, nearly always full of glee: you could see he was full of himself, because *he* was the winner, not the others. All that tension he'd talked about: was it really there? Yes, probably. But he certainly knew how to mask it. Something of an Italian trait, thought Nao: plenty of smiles and friends, but in the end it's *me* that wins, *me* that feeds on the applause and *me* that pockets the winnings. Anyone who acts like that has what it takes and so wins the race. He's won before it's even started, before even competing, and can only lose if something goes askew, otherwise *the winner wins*. That's how it is, and not just in sport. It's chemical, instinctive, electrical: if you go all out, you win, otherwise that negativism – which you didn't even realise you had – will influence the result and you'll come close to victory but won't clinch it. Something will snap and you'll lose by a few feet, your petrol will run out on the last lap. It's not bad luck. It's you that doesn't have the magic ingredient. Like all true winners, Agostini dominated for years. When you get to become a winner – and probably you're born one – you should, with a little intelligence and luck manage to stay at the top of the heap for years. That's how it always – or nearly – goes. No accidents, no problems: everything went as smooth as clockwork.

Take Agostini. He dominated for years without ever getting hurt, except towards the end of his career. They used to say that he won because he had the best motorcycle and raced against nobodies, which in a sense was true. He was the prodigy that blossoms once every ten years. All the others were also-rans, outsiders. The star gets the spotlight and the others only get the light that reflects off of him.

It's the same with boxing: until a worthy adversary who is as fearless and as strong as – or stronger than – him comes along, a champion fights unworthy foes. But that doesn't make him any less tough or diminish his greatness.

Nao was, he reflected, entering into the mindset of the Winner just a tad too much. He had wanted to remain detached from everything, especially him, the Winner. Why? Because it was a job. Just a job. He didn't want to start asking himself questions. All he wanted to do was tell the Winner's story and tell it as well as he knew how. And that essentially meant giving everyone exactly what they expected: the Winner his hagiography and the editor a book that would sell. Ah, but were the two things compatible?

NAO Wasn't this habit of last-minute arrival on the starting grid also a way of facing the moment of truth as late as possible?

GIACOMO Yes, it was. Because it really was the moment of truth. And those two or three minutes before the start in which you no longer had anything to do and could only wait seemed to last forever.

NAO Who were the people who stayed closest to you on the race Sunday?

GIACOMO At first I had my three or four trusted friends from Lovere who'd accompany me all over the show and even act as mechanics. Even after I became an official rider some of them stayed at my side. One name in particular springs to mind: Bonetti Giacomo, called The Boss. It was he who cleaned my helmet, prepared the basin of hot water to warm my feet when I had to do the day's second race – the 500 – because sometimes it was cold or maybe the rain had soaked my socks. He'd bring me veal cutlets and scrambled eggs made by his mother, who had a restaurant, or salami and bread from Lovere with which to make tasty sandwiches. He kept me going. It wasn't like today, with thirty-two different restaurants in the paddock area, each team with its own hospitality facility. You just got by as best you could. MV would stock its truck with a demijohn of wine and some cold cuts for the mechanics…

NAO Why are champions so often shadowed by this person who follows them around all the time? What does it mean?

GIACOMO There are times when you don't feel like being with a crowd, you just want to be with someone to whom you can say "Go and fuck yourself" or "Shut up!" or "Get my shoes please" – or just "Get the bloody shoes", without so much of the "please". He's perfectly aware you're not doing it out of haughtiness or spite, that you just need someone who knows you well, who's not going to get offended because you've asked him to pass you your leathers or because, when you were feeling edgy, told him to get a move on. If you're a real friend, if you really understand me then you know it's all said without any malice. I could relax because, for instance, he knew I wanted mineral water not tap water. He was a bit like a trusted mechanic: during pre-race preparation I'd beckon him over and he already knew he had to pass me first the helmet and goggles and then the gloves. He needed nothing explaining. It was all automatic.

NAO A reassuring presence then, that prevents you from feeling alone?

GIACOMO That as well: when it comes to the crunch you actually *want* to be alone – but with someone at your side who will stay quiet, someone who'll only exist when you want him to. And not everyone can accept this role. You might have a friend who's closer to you, but you choose the guy who understands you better, who's more helpful or knows exactly what you need because he's sharper. You require him to be there and not be there, to be there only when needed or otherwise stay silent – because you are not in the mood for chit-chat.

NAO Was the person already at your side in the morning? Was he with you throughout the race weekend?

GIACOMO Yes, yes. And then I used to go and see my mechanics and sit with them for a while because they made me feel calm. They'd explain that the bike was in tip-top condition, that they'd cleaned this and that, that they'd adjusted the carburetion and the bike was now even faster than it was the day before. It was all a way of making me feel comfortable, psyching me up. They'd say "I opened her up and found a dirty valve. We smoothed it beautifully for you...". They put me in a positive frame of mind, so I enjoyed hanging out in the paddocks with them. They were never far away. It was only when there were crowds of people that I'd go and hide, otherwise I'd be sat there on a wooden stool with them.

NAO Who were these mechanics?

GIACOMO Let's see: Magni, Mazza, Carrano, Castelli, Rosolino. They were the Holy Five, the ones who were always there. Later, towards the end, they were joined by Fiorenzo Fanali. There were others too, but those five were the ones. All I had to do was look at them and they instantly knew what I needed. This was why I complained when I moved to Yamaha, because they'd change the technicians every two months and send me new ones. They said they had to teach the others, that they all had to learn. But for me, who'd spent weeks explaining I wanted two loops of red tape around the throttle and a spiral of wire underneath to improve the grip, it meant explaining everything again to the new guys just two months later. I had to explain my habits, my flaws and so I had a bit of a go at them about that. The Japanese were lovely people, mind you, they'd work tremendously hard. But the guys at MV *knew* what I wanted: remember, just before a race you don't feel like talking, you clam up – or at least I did. It wasn't grumpiness, it was just that my head was full of thoughts and there was no desire to joke around. I only listened to what I was interested in and, with so many people jabbering at me, filtered out the rest. One minute later I'd have completely forgotten what they'd said because, while they were speaking I'd be thinking about the gear changes: fifth here, sixth there, here I'll slide it into first, then second...

NAO Were you obsessive when it came to setting up the bike?

GIACOMO Not too much, but everything had to be precise. Everything had to be perfect: if the gear lever was 3.2 mm then it had to be 3.2 mm - always. Take the length of the motorcycle, for instance: I'd get on one and then the other and say "Not this one". "What do you mean? They're the same!" they'd answer. "No, they're different". So out would come the tape measures and one would be 92.5 cm long and the other 92 cm long: if there was a difference of half a centimetre from the seat to the handlebar stem I'd feel it. It was a sort of sixth sense. When Hailwood tried my MV, he said, "Hey, you're racing with a different bike". "No", I replied, "the bikes are the same, it's just that I've adjusted mine and you haven't".

NAO Magni said, in fact, that they could set the bike up as they liked and Hailwood would still fly, that he didn't worry about the details whereas you were meticulous.

GIACOMO To beat Hailwood I had to have the bike at one hundred percent. Whether he, instead, had the bike at one hundred percent or seventy percent made no difference to him, he'd still clock up the same time: 1'10" with the bike sorted, 1'10" without the bike sorted. With me, a bike at seventy percent slowed me to 1'12", and only with the bike just right could I do 1'10". I wanted perfection. For example, the brakes had to be just right. When it rained I'd wrap red tape around the brake levers to keep the water out because on the long straits the water could get in and when you squeezed the lever it could jam. Since it had already happened to me, I checked out the brakes personally whenever it was wet. Hailwood, instead, didn't do a thing, because he was one of those racers who just grabs the bike and goes. He was just fast, that's all there is to it.

At this point the recording ended. When the next one began he could hear the background clatter of plates and cutlery. Nao remembered the first time he'd been to the Winner's home: he and the editor had been offered a sumptuous caviar and champagne supper. The last time they'd eaten together at his home it had been cheese sandwiches. But that's how it goes, work is work. You can't always pamper the people you're working with. It is, considered Nao, similar with women: you wow them to win them over but if you keep on doing it you spoil them - and end up ruining yourself. Capitalising on such initial investments was not as bad as some might believe: Nao remembered he used to use the same trick at school: study like mad the first two months of the year, impress the teachers with his diligence, then start coasting: by then they knew he was good, and so while he might finish the year on a downward note, nice and easy, his grades a tad lower than expected, his excellent reputation would still be intact. And if there was some snag, at the end of the year he'd deliver the knockout punch: with a perfect oral or written exam he'd amaze the teacher who'd had his doubts and set everything right. Like a piano concerto in which the thing you absolutely must get right is the end, the final notes: if you mess those up that's what the public will remember, even if all the rest was played to perfection.

Giacomo at eight months with his mother, Maria Vittoria, outside the Agostini family home at Cividate Camuno (Brescia).

Above: a four-year-old Giacomo Agostini treads the streets of his childhood.
Below: with his father Aurelio at Aprica at the age of six.

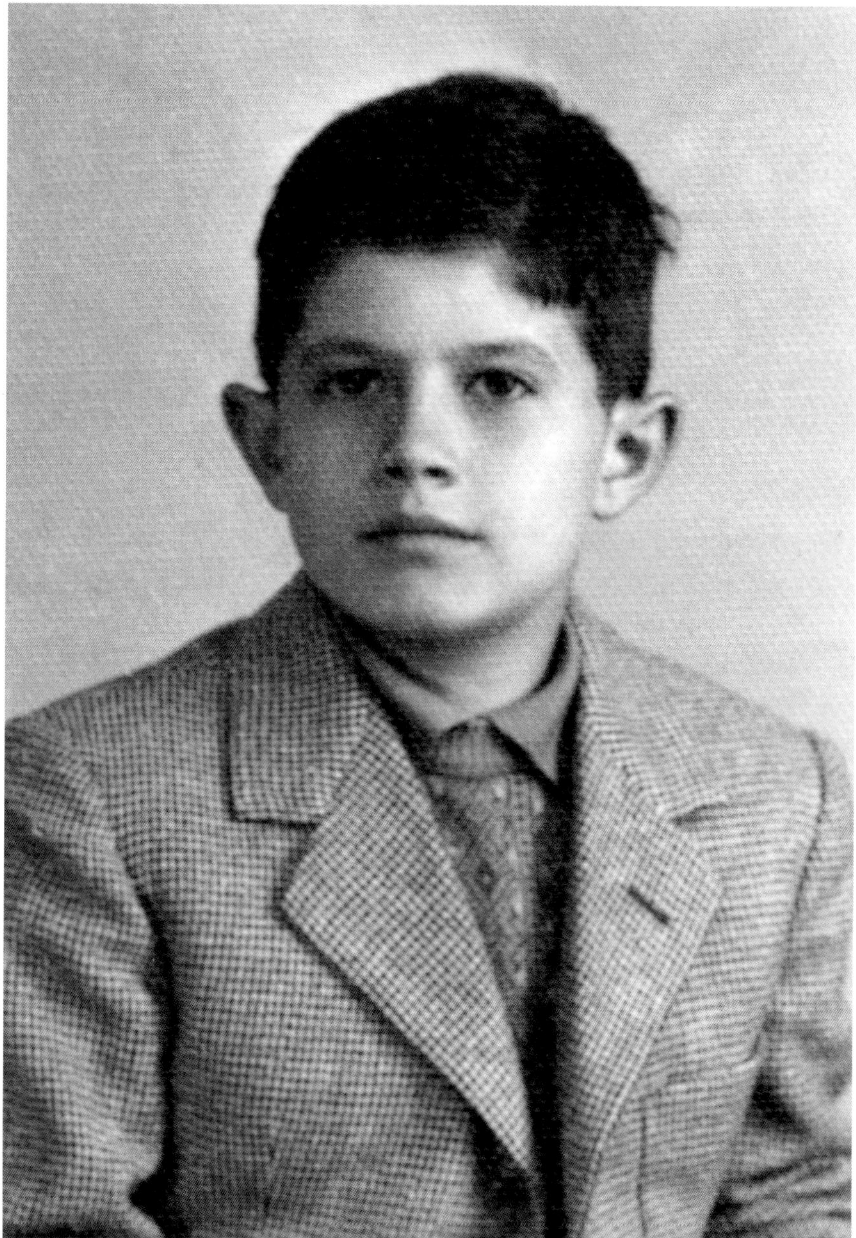

Giacomo the schoolboy: the fine-looking features are already those of the future champion.

Boating on the estuary of the River Oglio, where it flows into Lake Iseo:
the road around the lake would give him his first taste of motorcycling.

1953: Giacomo Agostini wins the first cup of his career in his very first race, the climb from Malegno to Borno. The motorcycle is a Moto Guzzi 250.

Sixties-style uphill racing technique: around the hairpins with one foot sliding on the asphalt to prevent side-skidding. The bike is a Morini 175 Settebello.

First races (with Morini). Above: the faithful friends who never left his side.
Below: at Ospedaletti in 1962 during the winner's lap of honour.

From private rider to official rider: Giacomo Agostini is soon taken on by the Morini team, which gave him a high-speed Settebello.

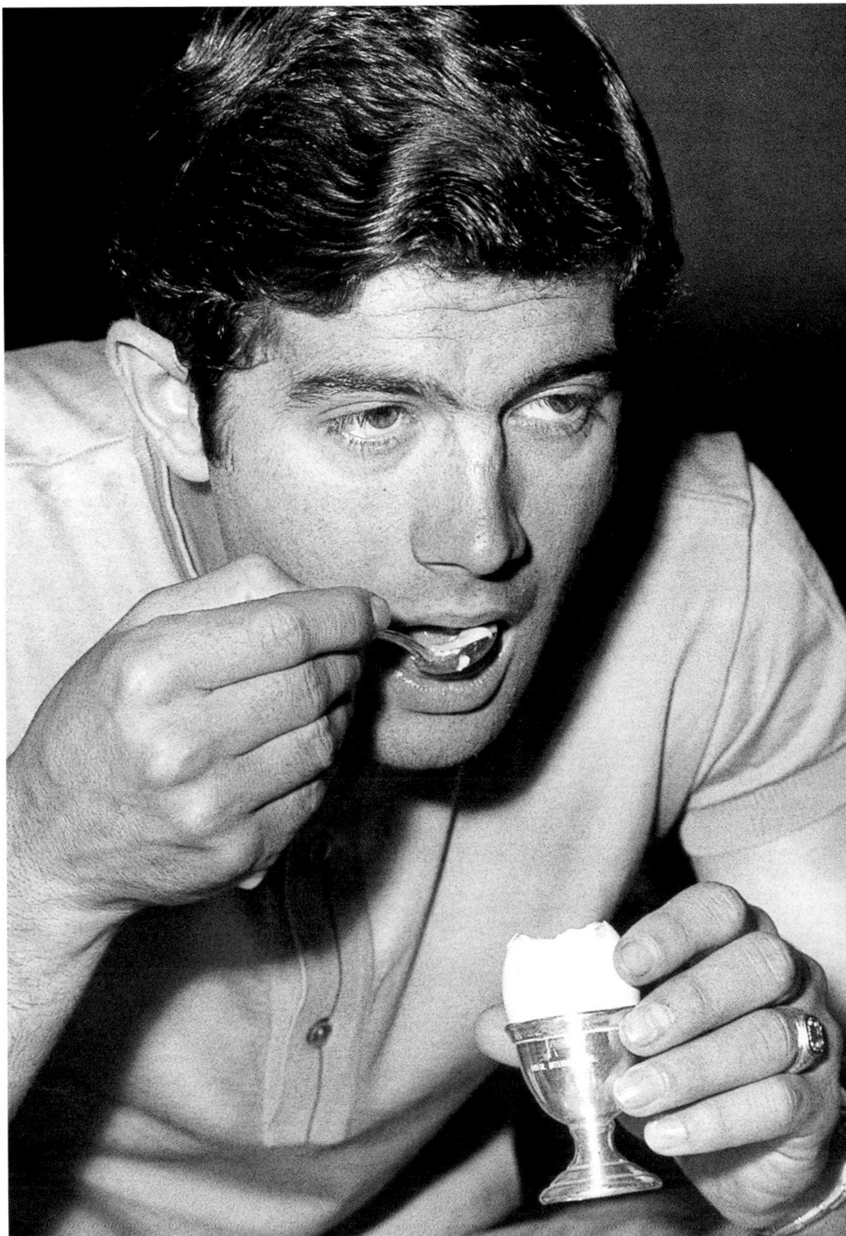

His morning egg-eating habit was learnt from Phil Read: the Englishman said it was why he won races, so Agostini, just in case, took up the same practice.

Rocketing around bends with the Morini 250 in 1964. With this motorcycle Agostini soon made a name for himself as an up-and-coming Italian talent.

National motorcycling and its enthusiastic following.
On the podium at Cesenatico: from left, Alfonso Morini (with the cup), chief mechanic Lambertini, Giacomo Agostini and Scagliarini.

From Morini to MV Agusta: in 1965 Agostini switched teams.
Here he is portrayed on the 4-cylinder MV 500, a bike he never really loved.

Above: victory celebrations (from left: Count Mario Agusta, Agostini and Count Domenico Agusta). Below: the MV riders flank the Agusta brothers.

Winning on inner-city circuits such as Riccione meant riding like this:
as close to the hay bales as possible to exploit every last inch of asphalt.

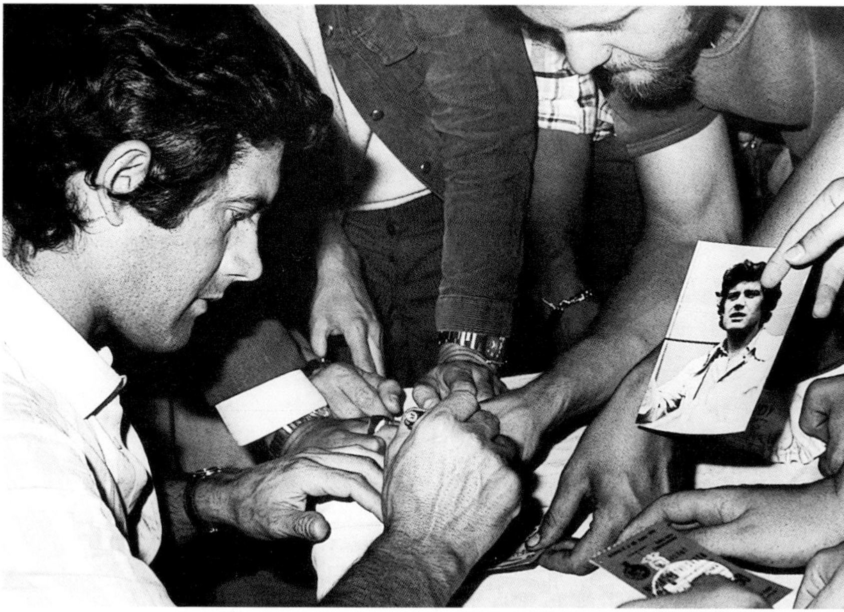

Above: with MV came the first big victories and Agostini's rise to stardom.
Below: a painting depicting the duel with Hailwood at the Sachsenring in 1967.

Agostini's only race on the twin cylinder MV 250, at the Alicante circuit in Spain:
once again, he was the first over the finishing line.

What a guy, eh, this Nao: always a bit calculating, always a bit aloof, always getting what he wants. A talent for opportunism that he was actually quite proud of.

GIACOMO The mechanics would bend over backwards for me. They might find some miniscule fault and say "I've put this right, I've put that right". They did it to relax me, to motivate me. "Today the bike's perfect, you'll see". They said it sincerely, so I'd think "Great, I've got a faster bike". Once, though, I was on the 4-cylinder 350 at Salzburg and Saarinen was slipping away from me by half a second, maybe even a full second, each lap. That night, back at the hotel, I was miserable. It was half past eight, it was raining, and there we were stuck in this pension, having dinner. I said "I can't see us winning tomorrow. No, it's not on, I can just *feel* the bike's not right". Mazza says "Oh, no, no". Magni: "What are you talking about. Honestly...". So Mazza, who looked after me like I was his pupil, said, "Guys, come on! Let's go and strip the engine for him!". The 4-cylinder! My friend Giacomo went to the hotel manager and asked if we could use a spare room – or perhaps even the hall. They stripped the engine right down and it's not like a 2-stroke, it's much more complicated. They started at ten-thirty even though they'd been up since six in the morning and finished at three-thirty in the morning. In the morning, before going to the circuit, I tried the motorcycle out on the road. It started perfectly, purring smoothly. "It's spot on. We checked everything and found the springs had gone a bit soft". Because I'd said the engine wasn't running as it should do, they checked it, found that the valves springs had weakened and replaced them with new ones: I usually revved at 14,500 rpm, but that morning, on the grid, the engine hummed at 14,800 rpm – and I went on to win. Mazza, in fact, at the end of the race, said: "You're a bloody fusspot, but when you notice something...". I had a feel for the bike and they knew it: if he's saying there's a problem then there is one. Poor guys, they worked their fingers to the bone: even after stripping that engine they were on their feet at seven – after working until three-thirty in the morning! Not all riders noticed problems like sloppy valve springs, but I knew that something wasn't right, I could *feel* it. When I was up on the podium they'd burst into tears too and think "We've worked ourselves senseless, but this sort of joy is priceless". They hadn't worked for nothing, they were proud to be with a rider who had noticed such a small problem - and plenty of others like it. They had faith in me, and if I said "Guys, something's up", they knew that something was. People will talk and talk but the truth is this: we were a team, we sought precision in everything and that was sometimes achieved with the aid of my gift for perceiving even the slightest alterations. The shock absorber isn't like it was before: they'd check and the travel would be two millimetres shorter. "How the hell did you notice that?", they'd say. "No idea, I was right though, wasn't I?". If my sixth sense said the engine wasn't running as usual, then it wasn't: when they got it back in the workshop, they would realise it wasn't like the others. It might be something minor, but it was there. Sure, the MV was magnificent, but the other makers weren't exactly slouches either: MV got the results it did because we trusted each other and worked as a team. When both Pasolini and I started winning in Italy I said "The world's a different place this year: we're not winning against Benelli because Pasolini's riding like the wind and he's got one hell of a bike!". Luckily for me, though, the race calendar soon took us abroad to the Nürburgring, and I was sticking a second and a half, maybe two seconds into Pasolini every lap: the point is that I could go like the clappers in front of a home crowd in Italy *and* abroad; to me it was practically the same thing, although Monza, of course, was special and really got me going. Pasolini instead, once outside his native Romagna, lost seconds because the fans weren't there to psych him up. For example, if we raced in Imola he'd fly away from me in a way that I would never have imagined – because I was riding like the devil myself. Then we went to the Nürburgring and he was two seconds a lap to the bad – and he knew the track well. The fact is that my speed didn't depend on where I was, whereas he, instead would do well here but not there, also because it was a demanding circuit. The bike was the same: we finished the race in Imola on the Sunday and left for the Nürburgring on Tuesday, giving the bikes little more than a clean. The difference was in *us*.

NAO Why did you find it so important to have the certainty of mechanical perfection?

GIACOMO Because it let me perform at one hundred percent.

NAO So you could only perform at one hundred percent if everything was in order?

GIACOMO I used to put a lot of effort into setting up the bike, and when it was one hundred percent then so was I – perhaps one hundred and ten percent. That was when the real Agostini, the great lap times, the victories against Hailwood came out: and that's how it had to be. I just couldn't ride properly with handlebars that were a little narrower or wider than was right for me. Oh, sure, I could ride: but only at ninety-nine percent.

NAO So the champion's duties also includes attention to detail...

GIACOMO Talent is a gift, but it isn't enough on its own. Lots of things make you a winner, a champion. Some say it's courage, but no, it's not that. I remember when I was a youngster: there was a guy from town who was fearless when it came to motorcycling. He did the Riviera, the loop around Lake Iseo and I reckon he had the edge on me because he would practically scrape up against the walls, slide in between lorries and more besides... His courage was undeniable. But if we then went to a circuit where you could go all out, he'd lose two seconds per lap. Becoming a champion requires many things: a touch of talent, sure, but also the intelligence to understand that this gift has to be nurtured, complemented by other things. I've met champions who have arrived at the top of the heap and then thought: "Right, now I can hit the discotheque, do this, do that". No, no. You need to be intelligent enough to understand the importance of preparation, that you need to make choices. For example, when I started racing there was Gilera; at Monza they offered me a contract that paid me twice as much as MV was offering but I still signed for MV Agusta because I sized things up and came to the conclusion that MV was a company with far greater resources behind it. So I signed for MV and accepted half as much money as I would have got with Gilera. It was my choice, and an important one, because if I'd gone with Gilera I might not have been world champion fifteen times. The winning champion is always with the winning bike, just as the winning bike will always be a magnet for the winning champion. Hailwood raced with Honda, and you know who they are, yeah? Hailwood competed on the MV Agusta, and were MV Agusta a bunch of nobodies? Rossi raced with Honda, not some Mickey Mouse motorcycle. Rossi's in a class of his own, but he's always raced with the top bikes. The same was true of Agostini. Some will say "Of course Valentino wins, he's got the best machine": they used to say the same about me. They're right too. But if we're given the best bikes it's because we've done something special to deserve them. When I started racing I was no-one. I lost a whole year waiting for my father to sign the authorisation slip because back then you needed your parents' approval even if you were eighteen, otherwise you had to wait until you were twenty-one. He said he'd never sign his son's death warrant: yet one day we were visiting a friend of his, a solicitor, who, on seeing me so down in the dumps, said to my father, "Give him permission: it's better to have him doing sport rather than hanging around doing nothing". The funny thing is that I later found out the solicitor thought I wanted to race bicycles, not motorbikes! Anyway, I left for my very first race together with a friend, a baker who doubled up as mechanic. I set off with my father's car, a rented trailer and a couple of sandwiches in my pocket. I came second. My first race, and I had come second! Everyone said, "Who the hell is this guy!?". Just before the race that gave me my first victory I had to buy a new tyre because I'd worn out the one I had in the qualifying laps. I didn't have the money for it so we had a whip-round: I paid in 500 liras, my friend another 500, his friend another 500 and so on - and that tyre gave me my first win. When it was over I was exhausted but as high as a kite; I celebrated in the van – a Giulietta – with the sandwiches, my friends and that hard-won winner's cup. So don't think it's always been a case of have-have-have. I've only ever "had" what hard work has given me. They didn't give me an official bike because my name was Agostini, you know. It was because I deserved it. I was just one among many, I'd started out so penniless that the thing I remember most about that period are the sandwiches I used to eat between one race and the next. My first motorcycle, a Morini Settebello, was bought, unbeknownst to my parents, on hire-purchase with my savings. I paid 7,000 liras a month. Nobody gave me anything, and why should they have done? I was unknown and I got no help from my father as he didn't want me to get involved in racing. Yet, after that first race, there I was on the podium – and on top of it come my third race! When, at Cesenatico, Morini let me try out the official bike, a Settebello, I was still a private rider. Now, Morini had three riders lined up to try out the motorcycle: on the basis of performance, one of them would get to keep it. Luckily, I went first; I went faster than anyone and set a new track record. At that point Morini's racing manager, Lambertini, said it was pointless letting anyone else try. He saw perfectly well what I'd done, the lap times, the track record and said, "That'll do. The bike's yours". The other two chaps didn't even get to sit on it because he'd been so impressed by my "system". Not my riding style or the slide-slipping on the bend, but the fact that I'd stopped to tweak the bike, then shaved a second off the lap time, then stopped again before hitting the track to establish a new record. What impressed him was the systematic way I'd managed to achieve that record.

Odd, thought Nao: the tape ended right after the word "record". A coincidence, but odd nevertheless.

As he'd listened to the tape he'd taken notes. One of the things he'd written was this: the Winner didn't just defeat his adversaries on the track, he even managed to make sure they didn't compete at all. He nipped them in the bud, just as adults stop children playing to prevent them destroying the family crystal.

Nao was tired. He decided to go to bed. As usual, he cleaned his teeth thoroughly, making circular movements with the brush and meticulously avoiding the gums so as not to make them sore.

Tape n° 2
The importance of being selfish

That evening he didn't feel like working on the Winner's book. The mere idea of doing so was enough to put him in a bad mood.

He left the office late and headed for the *trattoria* he went to whenever he felt like having a full evening meal. It was one of those fixed-price places, which had all but disappeared in the city centre but survived in the poorer districts. They were mainly open for lunch, catering to workers and passers-through, but a few stayed open in the evenings as well.

Half past-eight was lock-up time at the publishing house, and so whether you'd finished or not out you had to go. Just so as to remind you to shove off, they dimmed the lights for a few seconds. Nao wasn't generally one of those people who always hung on 'til the last moment, but he did work late quite often. And when they booted him out he'd always have a moan at whoever was on hand: except at that time there was no-one left as they'd all gone home hours before.

He took life as it came, and took it easy. But he wasn't a slacker: if something had to be done, Nao put his back into it. A young man without many merits - well, not *any* merits really, he would admit to himself - Nao had learned to live with himself. In fact, he liked things just as they were. He really *wanted* to be a nobody. He had never been, nor had aspired to be, a front-runner, a leader. His goal was to reach a low-level position of power so as to earn more, live more comfortably and take things easier at work, which was, and always would, as he knew, take the biggest slice of his life. His ambition, which wasn't so much an ambition as pure calculation, was to gain a better lifestyle, enjoy things a bit more and nestle himself more comfortably into the fold of the world that surrounded him.

However, Nao did have one thing going for him. When something needed finishing you could be sure he would finish it - and on time: he wasn't one to slip up. Meeting editorial deadlines was, after all, his job, and he sought to do it as well, obstinately and in as less an amenable way as possible. He behaved like corporal Asch, somewhat militarily, but when he did that he'd have to stifle his own laughter, almost as if he couldn't take his own military tone seriously.

He believed himself to be witty, but nothing could have been further from the truth. Instead he was a touch scurrilous, vulgar almost, as much in his way of speaking as in his dress sense. Ditto for his physical appearance: Nao wasn't by any means ugly, but he didn't look after himself at all. His lazily-chosen second-rate clothes were a shabby imitation of jacket and tie that his colleagues imposed on themselves. Since no-one had told Nao how to dress, he wore these clothes for his own personal pleasure; he looked more like a council clerk than the up-and-coming manager he sometimes felt like when he knotted his tie in front of the mirror. Like a clerk, he dressed with the same lack of enthusiasm, the same dourness. A shirt and a pair of jeans would have suited him better because his dark suit added years to his age. Although only in his thirties he already had an elderly air about him. He played at being worldly-wise, expert, the man-in-the-know: in any case the years were passing, so he really *was* maturing. He might have liked giving the impression of being an intellectual, seeing as he was a journalist and made his living out of words, but in truth he was as practical as can be, and you could see it the moment you looked into his eyes.

His trousers were tugged at his waist on account of a further weight gain. The shirt collar had to be kept unbuttoned otherwise it choked him, and the tie thus served the purpose of drawing the two collars together and was thus knotted nice and tight. They were never brightly-coloured ties with personality: they were, well, just ties.

Years of writing and correcting had not done his eyesight any good either: Nao wore glasses. His hairline was receding too: anyone who hadn't seen him for five or six years would have had trouble recognising him. He looked out of shape, puffy with thinning hair. It would only be fair to say that he'd aged beyond his age, that he looked older than he was. All this, of course, was not exactly in his favour. Personally, he attributed his physical demise to stress, overwork; but the harsh truth was that he neglected himself, that he couldn't care less. His selfishness – because he *was* selfish – came out in other ways, but definitely not as narcissism.

His thoughts wandered back to Agostini: no, he wouldn't be

working on the book that evening. He didn't feel like it.

He wasn't behind with the work: as always he'd laid out a timetable and stuck to it. He'd never missed a deadline, and anyone who messed about with *his* deadlines found themselves in deep trouble, because Nao had worked hard to build a reputation for reliability. If anyone was going to fess up, it wasn't going to be him. So he could well afford the luxury of eating out and a drink in the pub. On schedule, he knew it was in the bag. What harm was there in a break every now and then?

Like plenty of other such places, the *trattoria* always offered the same menu. The pasta was overdone, the tomato sauce tinned. As usual he ordered a *scaloppina* with a little *insalata verde*, which was exactly that, no more and no less - the sort you get in those ready-to-eat packs from the supermarket. The house red was the usual table wine of unknown origin. Yet all this simply made Nao feel at home. In fact, he felt more at home in dumps like this, real dives, than he did in his real home, where the fridge was eternally empty, where he only went to sleep, the sad place he escaped to on Friday evenings and to which he never invited friends or women.

After dinner he went for a spin in the car. He stopped off at a *birreria* and sat down to a quiet drink. He knew the bartender and had a quick chat with him at the counter. Afterwards he moved to a table, and continued drinking on his own as he observed the other customers. For the most part they were groups of friends. There were also a few couples, who, like all passion-struck couples, were glued to each others' eyes as if nothing else mattered at all. Nao, of course, had experienced the same feelings himself, and the spectacle of people convinced the world would end that very night, that their lives went no further than the person in front of them, inevitably aroused his curiosity. They made him feel sentimental, although it was hard to imagine someone like Nao getting sentimental about anyone as he was too rational and shrewd to let himself go. He'd tasted life on his own and had found it tough: he understood that if you don't pull your finger out you can die of starvation - and no-one will come knocking to ask you what the problem is.

After the second beer he paid, left, got back in his car and drove around some more. It was late but not too late. He loved this part of the city by night, these poorly-lit outskirts that were a sort of no-man's land (or, rather, strong-man's land). The way the men and women - the pimps and hookers, the petty criminals, the kids on the run from themselves - lived out their nights intrigued him. For a while he'd frequented the fast-food and beer kiosks, but they were too dangerous; a fight with broken bottles or even handguns might break out between Albanian immigrants, so he'd stopped going. In a pub it was different: it was a closed environment in which just about everyone knew each other. Not the kiosk: it belonged to the guy who parked his souped-up black Mercedes on the kerb. It was like with certain women: it's not the first one to arrive who gets them, it's the strongest. The women were nice enough: it's just that they were programmed to go for that sort of guy, only felt at ease with the rough-edged men who made them feel female and something of an object.

Nao observed everything and tried to keep out of trouble. At night the strangest things happened, the oddest creatures came out. Sure, it was low life, but it was life: instinctive and animalistic. Zero sentiment, plenty of action. Here, countless lives ran aground on the rocks because the nightlife doesn't last long: it burns you up, so you either save yourself or die. And the means of destruction was nearly always alcohol. Drugs too, but Nao had never set foot inside that particular world. Alcohol, instead, he knew. Not that he ever overdid it himself. But he had observed the rest of the world, glass in hand, crumbling apart. Lives that had, until then, been built attentively and which – for whatever reason (or no reason) - had imploded.

Women, and plenty of fragile men too, were the ones who went under. They sucked at the bottle until they no longer had any idea who they were or what they should do. People who two years previously had been sipping after-work aperitifs with their friends and were now as bloated as drowned corpses, white and puffy with glazed eyes and a breath that stank of alcohol. Nothing more could be done at this point, it was over. Kaput! Everything had already been lost and only death would save them.

They were all people who had let themselves go, who only had the nerve to go out at night, because at night all humanity goes a bit to pot, not just the portion with the scorched synapses.

As he waited at the traffic lights an old prostitute came up to his window. "*Ciao bello*, what are you up to?", she purred. He gazed at her and replied, "Matilde, it's me, Nao. Don't you recognise me anymore? What are you playing at? Are you trying it on with me too?". While embarrassment is difficult to arouse in a worn-out whore of fifty, her face rippled with unease: Nao burst out laughing and waved good bye as the lights changed to green. Yep, he liked that world and its sick inhabitants. Without knowing why, he felt at ease with them. More than in the editorial office or the daytime world, where everything was clean and perfect – but wasn't.

As he drove he recalled, for no particular reason, the time that a woman had wet herself at the bar: totally drunk, she had laughed heartily as she had done so. She'd then fallen over and soaked herself in her own urine, and had burst into tears as she had, perhaps, in a moment of lucidity, realised what she was doing. To look at her you'd have thought she was quite respectable. Then Nao remembered the Chinese bartender who, without a word, without swearing or getting angry, had wiped up that woman's urine with a grimy cloth and had squeezed it into a bucket of dark water. Maybe, considered Nao, that was why he liked that smelly gone-to-the-dogs world.

A glance at his watch told him it was late. He was tired of driving around. He did a U-turn and went home, which was pretty close anyway.

The following evening he was ready to have another go at the Winner's book. After all, it wasn't going to write itself. So he sat at the table in his underpants, ate the Cantonese rice and almond chicken he'd bought on the way home and then sat down to listen to the tape…

NAO How were you as a child?

GIACOMO Pretty lively. My head was full of motorcycles, I had loads of toy cars and stuff like that and I knew, as soon as I could think, that I wanted to race motorbikes. I got my first moped at just nine, a roller-driven Aquilotto Bianchi. When they told me that I'd be getting the moped the next day, there I was standing outside the dealer's at six in the morning – even though they didn't open 'til eight. Once I got it I just took off for the day, completely forgetting that I was supposed to go home. My parents were worried sick of course, but I was just so excited that I didn't even realise the day had gone by and I hadn't drunk or eaten a thing. The joy of riding that moped just swept all before it. You can imagine the scene when I finally got back… Mum and Dad knew I'd picked up the bike and hadn't heard from me since… So I got a few slaps for that, and quite rightly! I was old enough to know that they'd be concerned. Even then, with that moped, I wanted to race: yes, the thought was always there. I used to read the sports papers, but there wasn't the flood of information you get today: back then it was difficult to get hold of the details. You had no idea who made the special brakes or leathers, who made the racing accessories for the bikes. It wasn't easy to find out stuff like that, especially if you lived in a backwater like I did. To try out bigger bikes I'd try anything... Because this was an Aquilotto, and when it rained the roller would slip and I had to bloody pedal! There was this kid who was older than me and had a Guzzi, an Airone to be precise. To try it out this is what I'd do: he had a crush on my good-looking cousin so I used to say to him, "Look, I'll help you go out with her, but while you're with her you leave me your bike, all right?". I used to zip off on it for half an hour, something I was certainly too young to do, but back then there weren't too many police cars about. Even though I was still a kid, I caught people's eye: a certain Stocchetti, local baker and died-in-the-wool racing enthusiast, had seen me riding and invited me to take part in a rally on a Guzzi 250. Without saying a word to my parents I accepted and raced in the Malegno-Borno, which later became an "uphill climb" race. When I reached the square at Borno I couldn't stop - because I couldn't touch the ground! So I just kept riding round in the hope that someone would realise my predicament and step in. There was this carabiniere, his eyes bulging in disbelief, who just kept staring at me, a ten-year-old kid on a motorcycle... I mean, I could only just reach the footrest... I kept trundling round and noticed a step, so I drew up to it and stopped. Then the *carabiniere* helped me get off, amazed this child could ride such a large bike: he didn't even bother booking me. There's even a photo from the event. And that was when I won my very first cup, which I still have today. I haven't stopped dreaming or racing since.

NAO Motorcycles aside, what do you remember of life before the age of nine? What sort of kid were you?

GIACOMO Just like all the others: I used to cycle all over the place and play with beer or orangeade caps: we'd stick picture-cards of famous cyclists such as Coppi, Bartali, Magni, Bevilacqua in them, cover them with a bit of glass and then putty it to finish. Then we'd make a track and throw the caps to see who came first. I was quick-witted, certainly not a quiet kid: I was a bit of a tearaway. Once, on my Dad's Fiat 500 *Giardiniera*, I came up with a device that let me open the sun roof and managed to make a copy of the ignition key. When he got back from the office and took a kip I'd putter off for a spin. I was only ten or eleven! Of course, I know now just how much trouble I risked getting my father into, even though nothing happened... Remember, there was no traffic to speak of at the time and I was always on country roads. No, I was no quiet kid, and I lived and breathed motorcycles. Like all the other boys I went around on my bicycle, had my toy cars, trucks and - of course, motorbikes.

NAO A rider you were a fan of, someone you wanted to be like?

GIACOMO When I was a bit older I was a fan of Carlo Ubbiali and Tarquinio Provini, but it wasn't like today: there were no motorcycling magazines, no televised races, so I didn't really know much about it. And I didn't get much contact with the environment anyway 'cause by Dad wasn't a mechanic, his job had nothing to do with motorcycles. Yet despite all this I desperately wanted to race. I knew very little about the racing world, most of it gleaned from browsing through the *Gazzetta dello Sport*, but I was very aware of Ubbiali and Provini and their skills. I used to say to myself, "Wouldn't it be wonderful to grow up to be racers like them". And I'd cry when I said it. Indescribable feeling would run through me. As I said previously, the passion didn't arrive after thinking about or trying other things: I started thinking about motorcycles as soon as I could think- I've never though about anything else.

NAO Tell me about your family.

GIACOMO Mum was a housewife, Dad was a Lieutenant Colonel in the infantry; during the war he'd been stationed in Chieri, towards Turin, then at Abbazia, then the Italian sector of Yugoslavia. He'd had a timber yard, but it was burnt down during the war. In Val Camonica, where we lived, he got a post as town clerk and, in the meantime, set up an earth-moving company to excavate material from river banks. He'd studied economics at university but stopped just a few exams short of graduation, perhaps because of the war, I couldn't say. Anyway, his earth-moving and transport business did all right and as a result we moved, a few years later, to the Oglio estuary, on the shores of Lake Iseo, on the Bergamo side. From the age of thirteen, that's where I lived, in Lovere.

NAO How was your like back then?

GIACOMO When we were at Cividate Camuno, my father was town clerk at the small town of Bienno. He had a car and a motorcycle, a *Galletto*. When it rained he took the car, leaving the *Galletto* at home – with me taking it out on the roads of course. Dad always asked me, "Who taught you how to ride?". "No-one, no-one". I loved motorcycles so much that all I had to do was look and observe and I would learn, just like that.

NAO What did your father leave you with? What memories?

GIACOMO I was aware that he thought the world of me. If he was going somewhere he'd often take me along, and I learnt a lot from him, especially when he went off on business. We'd inherited some land from my grandparents, we had sharecroppers and he'd take me – in the car or on the back of his motorcycle – to see the cows and chickens, and we'd come away with fresh milk and eggs. I've often thought that it would be interesting to try living like that, as most people did about sixty or seventy years ago. Well, for a week anyway, as they still used to wash themselves in tubs, after boiling the water. It would be great though, wouldn't it?... Yes, he taught me a lot. Later on, when I had to choose between a pro contract with MV or Gilera, I fancied the latter because the bike looked better. My father said, "No, always stay with the strongest, the biggest: MV build helicopters, and that takes technology". So I signed with MV, and it was the right choice. Yet the decision had largely been taken by my father; after all, I was barely out of boyhood and lacking in experience. I learnt how to do business from him: he was cultured, calm, didn't smoke or drink. It was just that he didn't have anything to do with the world I was so eager to get into: he had a motorcycle but knew nothing about it. There was no family motorcycling tradition, relatives who were champions. Although there was aunt Agnese, Mum's sister, who loved anything with engines and had, at the time, a souped-up Abarth. Perhaps I got it from her. But it was hard going. I got no help at all. No-one told me where to go or what to do. It was my stubbornness that kept me going. Others would have given up along the way.

NAO So your father, Aurelio, taught you how to make a decision and negotiate a deal.

GIACOMO Yes. He bought and sold excavators, and as I travelled around with him on his business trips I picked things up. When I had to negotiate a contract he'd suggest the plan of action.

NAO And your mother Maria Vittoria?

GIACOMO When it came to my decision to race she put up less of a fight than Dad did, perhaps because she'd already seen, with her sister, just how obstinate a person with the racing bug could be. She never worried too much really and had lots of faith in me. My father, instead, was more apprehensive.

NAO What sort of relationship did you have with your mother? What sort of mother was she?

GIACOMO Not too strict. A normal Mum, I reckon: a good housewife, a great cook who knew all grandma's recipes. There was nothing pretentious about her. I don't recall any earth-shattering events, it's not as if we argued much. She loved her children and often let us get our own way. Whether we worked hard at school or not was a problem she delegated to my father. If we messed up there, we'd get the bollocking from him. She just let us get on with our lives. She wasn't very demanding. My three brothers were simply left to live. She had her work cut out for her, mind. I was the oldest of the four.

NAO What are your brothers called. How old are they?

GIACOMO After me came Gabriele, who's five years younger, then Mauro, ten years younger than me, then Felice, three years younger again.

Nao stopped the tape to go to the toilet. He got up and went off to urinate. Whenever he was sat down for a long time his visits to the bathroom became frequent. In the editorial office he'd shuttle back and forth constantly. Yet when he was on the move he'd go maybe only twice a day.

What on earth would he say, he mused, if someone asked him about his own mother? How long would he talk about her?. Nao had been taken aback by the sheer ordinariness of the Winner's replies. Perhaps Nao had expected exceptional stories, exciting recollections or sharp-edged imagery. But no, all had been normal in the life of 'Ago', apart from the races and the victories: they, instead, were exceptional, and his memory of those was precise down to the last detail.

But aren't we all a bit like that? Don't we all remember the things we want to, the things that gave us joy because they turned out exactly as we hoped they would?

Nao too, he suspected, would have had little to say about his mother in the unlikely event that anyone asked him: he'd had a perfectly normal, nice enough childhood. He'd rather have spoken about something he'd wanted to do and had done, although unlike the Winner, Nao didn't have any great ambition. He'd become a journalist by chance: an older cousin was in the profession and had introduced him to the world of automobiles. Nao had felt in place there and slowly began to make his own way, smiling at everyone and talking behind everyone's backs, being friends to everyone and hating everyone. Hate, not money, made the world go round. Hate brings out the best in you, and if your best coincides with your worst, it's just coincidence or, rather, a necessity, an indispensable refuelling pit-stop on the road to success.

NAO What does it mean to grow up far from a big city, on the shores of Lake Iseo?

GIACOMO Depends on your temperament. Outside the big towns it's all different, much more so in my day than it is now. For example, to get to Brescia we wouldn't drive as we were unsure about negotiating a big city by car. Instead, we took the train that passed through Val Camonica. The train was used a lot. Going into town was exciting, but I felt a bit awkward looking at all those nice shops, the smartly-dressed people. In the small villages and towns of my day there was no luxury and no taste; now, even if you live in the tiniest village, people will, through TV and other media, see and know about everything… We had two pairs of short trousers each – and that was all. When we went into a large town and saw everyone looking spiff we felt humbled. City and country were two different worlds. Later on, thanks to my father who had given me a Giulietta Sprint, I started driving into Milan. It was 1961, a period in which I was the only one of my age to have my own car. If I ate out in Milan I'd hide that car, I wouldn't want people to see it. I was embarrassed, shy: I didn't want to be seen around Milan with a Giulietta Sprint. I'd park it a couple of blocks away then walk to where I was going.

NAO What gave you the will to win, the drive for success?

GIACOMO Sheer, unbridled zeal for the whole thing. Remember, it was me against everyone: no-one helped me, I didn't have friends who went to the races and took me with them. Only once did my father take me along, when I was already fifteen: it was at Milano Marittima and he took me because I wouldn't let up about it. I was in the same hotel as Provini: I had so much I wanted to say to him but when I saw him I just dried up and couldn't utter a word. I said to myself, "I want to be like him. I want to be a champion too". Before starting my career I'd seen just two or three races. Once, at Monza, I was crawling head-first under the fence (the track was immediately on the other side of it) when I felt myself being dragged backwards: two policemen had hold of my legs. I had practically wriggled onto the track, on the Lesmo chicane.

NAO How did you imagine the life of a champion? Was it a just vague idea or did you have some specific imagery, a daydream?

GIACOMO In my mind's eye I was on the motorcycle, on the podium. I'd have done anything to race. I got up in the morning and thought about racing: I wanted nothing else. I wasn't like most of my friends who said, "Come on, lets take the bike, go over the Stelvio (a mountain pass in the Alps) and tour for a day or two". No, I couldn't have cared less about cruising for three or four hours. I'd take off for half an hour, do the Riviera with the footrest skimming the tarmac and return with the exhaust pipes fuming: that was how I got my kicks. To me happiness meant going full throttle, leaning into the bend as much as possible, scraping exhaust and engine on the ground, feeling my leg touch the asphalt. I was interested in going all-out, not doing a tour to, I don't know, Sanremo. Doing something like that didn't cross my mind, I wasn't interested in it.

NAO Do you think it's fair to say that your boyhood was largely a long wait, a prelude to your racing career?

GIACOMO I'd go to school and daydream about motorcycles. I wasn't a diligent pupil. I'd say "What am I doing here, what good is it doing me, I want to race motorbikes". One day I told a teacher, "I come to school because I have to, but I couldn't care less because I know I'm going to do a different sort of job" I didn't think about my education, about culture: I just thought I was wasting time.

NAO Was it a period of happiness or sadness?

GIACOMO I was a boy and did what all boys did, with the same enthusiasm. The mischief-making, swimming in the River Oglio... But in addition to all that I had my motorcycling, my racing obsession. They all used to make fun of me, even my father, and say "Where do you think racing's going to get you? Can't you see you'll be up against the best, the champions?". "I want to try", I'd reply. "Can't you see they're all pros? What's the point in trying?". And I'd say: "They must have been nobodies at first, and like me, they must have had their dreams".

NAO Help me to understand the sort of person you were before you started racing.

GIACOMO Before doing proper races I did obstacle races (a slalom between cones organised in village squares). Once, at the Sunday school, there was this obstacle race, but I didn't feel like going in for it. A friend of mine, Italo, who's always been an enthusiast and extremely supportive of me, a guy who knew how to ride a motorcycle but not too well, had signed me up for the race. Oddly, I didn't want to do it, I felt shy. But when I noticed that one of the participants had only one leg I told myself, "If he can do it, so can I". I won: first overall. After that, there I was, every Sunday, out doing those races organised by the Sunday schools: a few years later my father bought me a Guzzi Lodola 175 and that was when my real race training began, because I'd be out on that bike from morning to night. I even went to school on it, and looking back, I did things that would, shall we say, be inadvisable. I'd head out and do thirty kilometres of Riviera, the footrests and exhausts sparking against the tarmac. Every now and then I'd overtake a road train: sometimes I'd overtake the trailer and then realise there wasn't time to overtake the tractor as well, so I'd slip in between the two and cruise along until there was room to pass. I'd go at full throttle along the Riviera, a road just three and a half metres wide with the lake on one side and a rock wall on the other. It was lethal: if anything came the other way the carriageway was taken up. So you really had to squeeze over on as much as possible and the slot for the bike couldn't have been more than fifty centimetres wide. I did things on that road that make me think Jesus keeps a special eye out for motorcyclists... I escaped death a thousand times. Once, at Lovere, I went into a right-hand bend at full throttle. A lorry was halfway round the bend, slowly turning left into a parking area. I saved myself by riding up onto the pavement between lake and road. It might have been forty-five or fifty years ago but I remember it well because I went back home fully aware that I was lucky to be alive. Afterwards I was shaking like a leaf and had, perhaps for the first time, stared death in the face. Luckily no-one had been coming the other way and there was that stretch of pavement to let me off the carriageway. If the lorry had been three feet further forwards I'd have killed myself there and then.

NAO What did you think about when you did all those miles?

GIACOMO It was pure joy, a delight.

NAO Didn't you think about anything?

GIACOMO No, I was focussed on the riding, observing the asphalt, looking out for other people. I was very careful.

Yes, thought Nao, he rather liked Agostini. Sometimes he hated him too, exactly because he was a winner, a nauseating, useless winner: he usually liked failures - and their failings. He was fascinated by those that fall so far they never get up again. Yet the Winner had charm, a certain savoir-faire. His opportunism, his pragmatism were magnetic. His success caught everyone's attention, Nao's included. His meticulousness, which in Nao's eyes made him smaller, had been a necessary ingredient in the triumph of winning more than anyone has ever done in motorcycling. And when he understood that he felt oddly drawn to him, wanted his smile, his attention: because he was the Winner, the *campionissimo*, the miracle rider, the Latin lover. He was Giacomo Agostini, the legend. A legend built on particulars, attention to detail, a spirit of self-preservation, parsimony, a smooth way of moving through the racing world (almost as if he were above it all, considered Nao: like all true champions, it was as if he looked down on the world, gracing mere mortals with his presence every now and again as occasion demanded), skilled networking, sharp decision-making, a capacity to take risks without losing sight of the limits. Did any of this diminish his status of champion? No, thought Nao. No, all these things made him the champion he was.

Talent, of course, was also one of those ingredients, and the Winner had it in profusion. Without it you don't slap the competition around for years. Everyone compared Agostini to Mike Hailwood, who, for many, was the *greatest* rider in the history of motorcycling. And if he was it was because of his talent, the fact that he rode like lightning whatever machine he sat on. He flew - even though he drank, went to bed late and burned the candle at both ends. At forty he had the weathered face of a man of sixty (the Winner, instead, looked eternally boyish. Even now, in his sixties, he had the bright-eyed face, sharp gaze and quickness of speech of a boy; only his early morning voice betrayed a hint of tiredness). Hailwood was liked by everyone: for being the bad boy of motorcycling, for his all-genius-and-recklessness approach. The Winner, instead, was a calculator, someone who didn't gamble, who made the right choices and did it all with a smile, brilliantly, cleverly. Not everybody likes this: people also want cursed heroes who die young and leave a legacy of legend, not just a long list of results and victories. The champion who survives is respected, the rash, gifted one who dies young is loved. It's inexplicable and perhaps incomprehensible, but it's one of those things decided in the gut, not the head. Like love for instance: a physical thing, that cannot in its absence be described in words. Love is eye contact, fleeting caresses, an odd sensation of hollowness, muscles taught with emotion. It is feeling. Hailwood was feeling and Agostini was reasoning. yet this does not make the former greater than the latter. Quite the contrary, thought Nao, if numbers mean anything in this world: and by God they do. They are, quite simply two different people and two very different kinds of champion.

Nao had been told the following story by an elderly man. As a boy, he had been at the Lesmo bend at Monza, watching the 1967 Italian GP. A few laps into the race there was a serious accident. Race leaders Hailwood (on a Honda) and Agostini (on an MV) were not involved. When they came round to where the accident had happened they were travelling at full throttle. Hailwood eased off the gas, slowed up and stood on the footrests to see what had happened, twisted the throttle wide open and roared right through the smoking chaos of the aftermath; Agostini, also travelling at full speed, eased off, braked and stood up to look, then dropped two gears and slowed right down, chugging gently through the accident area and only opening the throttle when he was past it. What are we to make of this? That one was a madman and the other not? That one was courageous but not the other? One a legend and one not? No, none of these, thought Nao. The story simply illustrated why Agostini took Hailwood's place at MV and dominated for ten years without hardly ever getting hurt. And why Hailwood abandoned motorcycling at the peak of his career to race cars: he was seriously injured in a crash, returned to motorcycling to perform as magnificently as ever and then lost his life in a car crash near his home caused by a lorry driver[1].

NAO Tell me about the first girlfriends.

GIACOMO Fair enough. At seventeen I fell head-over-heels in love with a girl who, although only twenty-four, seemed old to me. I used to go and pick her up in the afternoon or towards evening. Once I got a puncture on the way, but I really wanted to get there and so sat on the tank to take the weight off the rear wheel. The bike skated all over the place but I made it in the end... It was a classic boy's crush... She used to tell me not to race as it was dangerous. I told her I couldn't have cared less, that I wanted to race motorcycles because it was the most important thing I had and everything else took second place. "What?", she said. "You say you love me and then...". "Yes, yes", I went on, "I am in love with you – but the motorcycling comes first". The relationship fizzled out because I started racing seriously and travelled the world: and I was totally ab-

NOTE:[1] Born in 1940, Mike Hailwood (GB) won nine World Championships in the 250, 350 and 500 cc classes between 1961 and '67 and a total of 76 Grand Prix races. He won 14 Tourist Trophies on the Isle of Man, the last in '79. In '69 he started racing cars and in '72 took the European Formula 2 title. He competed in 50 Formula 1 GP races. In 1974 an accident at the Nürburgring interrupted his career. He died in 1981.

sorbed by it all and forgot about her. It wasn't like today: with a mobile phone in your pocket it's all so much easier.

NAO What was her name?

GIACOMO I'm not saying that. I don't want to name names. Let's say she was called Baby. Let's say they were all called Baby.

NAO Then you met Nicoletta, right?

GIACOMO I liked Nicoletta enormously, yet it was purely platonic. She was a student at Milan, her parents would have her chauffeured there so she could follow her courses. She was fantastic, wonderful, very upper crust. And I was the motorcyclist, the poor boy. Because that's how I was seen at the time, and maybe I felt that way too: she was in Milan, dressed well, studied, knew the "right" people - and I didn't. Yet I still have very fond memories. I'd have to say that it was more infatuation than love. With "Baby" there was love because we spent time together. With Nicoletta we met back up years later, both married by then, and told each other of our long-distance ardour, made up of glances. But to be honest, once I was racing I forgot about everything, couldn't have cared less about anything else.

NAO Love without sentiments?

GIACOMO Being able to race meant everything to me, there was nothing to compare with the satisfaction and joy of competing. I travelled, had a whole new world to discover. I'd started off as a kid and had done everything on my own, the commitment was total and made me forget about the rest.

NAO Your love life always took second place to your motorcycling career: when did it start to become more important?

GIACOMO When I stopped racing. But I wouldn't say it was "second-place". It was, quite simply, my second commitment. After these first crushes I started travelling and realised things had changed: I knew people, had friends in Holland, Germany, Belgium and Australia. It was no longer a schoolboy crush and I had girlfriends here and there.

NAO Did you live with anyone else before getting married?

GIACOMO Before marriage I lived with three other women. I was with one eight years, another four and about two and a half with the last one. Then I left the motorcycling world, met Maria in 1987 and married her the following year.

NAO All said and done, what do you think you've learnt about women?

GIACOMO A woman can make a man's life complete, fill an

emptiness that can't be plugged any other means. Yet maintaining a balanced relationship is no easy task because men tend to want to keep control; still, at the end of the day it's the woman, especially if she's a smart one, who keeps control – and I don't mean in an overbearing manner. If she's helpful and intelligent she'll succeed, to an extent, in getting you to do what she wants. A woman who returns your love will give enormous happiness, and if she's sharp she'll help your career along as well. The flip side is that she can also ruin it for you. With the woman I lived with for eight years I was lucky: she let me get on with what I wanted, didn't interfere one iota with my career or professional decisions, while I saw other riders influenced and ruined by women who thought they had taken hold of the situation but simply weren't up to the job. Although I lived with her for eight years I never ever thought we'd get married or have children; we both knew it would end one day, it was something that had been hanging in the air since we started seeing each other, not least because she was married. And as time went by we began to think it was right she should bring up her children and stay with her husband. But because we loved each other we just kept putting off the day of reckoning. We were happy together: a woman is essential to your life and can help you to success simply by seeing that you're utterly focussed and not asking questions, not making you cross, obstructing you or doing anything else that might damage your career.

NAO How much selfishness do you think is needed to make a relationship work?

GIACOMO Depends on the sort of person you are. While I respect other people's point of view, I've always wanted to decide things myself. At the end of the day, though, yes you do have to be selfish, whether you have an understanding partner or one who seems to be against you all the time. A woman - as happened to me - who draws you into an argument about you eating food she doesn't approve of just thirty minutes before the race: I mean, how can you honestly want to discuss something like that when you know your man is risking his life out there… Other women tried to alter my way of doing things more nicely, others just let me get on with it. I saw some riders bickering before the race, even scrapping with their girlfriends just before the start: women like that simply didn't understand what was at stake. It takes intelligence to understand what a rider's going through at times, especially just before the start when nerves, the will to win and the very real possibility of death all combine to rack up the pressure. As a woman you have to be intelligent, understand he's in a non-standard situation and provide support. The woman I was with for eight years would listen to me before the race, even if I was talking rubbish, because she knew what was at stake. I wasn't going off to play snooker, you know. Snooker's a fine game, but at most you lose the match, not your life. I was racing motorcycles.

NAO What period of your career did the relationship coincide with?

GIACOMO We were together from 1969-70 to 1977 if I remember rightly. Her name was Lucia.

NAO Did the other women you lived together with come before or after Lucia?

GIACOMO After.

NAO Would you say you were a selfish person?

GIACOMO Yes, somewhat, I'm quite selfish, but not in everything. My job made me so, because you can only give it your all if you have it all: the tyres, the mechanics, the best bike.

NAO What are you not selfish about?

GIACOMO In things that don't interest me the way motorcycles do. For instance I love sweets and cakes, and I don't mind sharing them with you. I love races too, but in that regard I'm not ready to share *anything*: if you want a spare part or a tyre for the race you won't get it from me. I'm possessive of my stuff: If you want to borrow my car or motorcycle just to go for a spin I won't let you have it. Since I'm something of a perfectionist, I don't want my stuff being damaged. For example, I do lots of things myself because I'm afraid other people are going to mess them up for me. I'll go and buy things myself 'cause I'm convinced they're going to come back with the wrong stuff. I'll wash the car at home because I'm worried the carwash will score the paintwork: first I douse it with cold water, then hot water, then shampoo it once, then twice… It's the same with women. If you love her you're selfish, because you want her all to yourself: if you don't love her you're neither selfish nor jealous.

Nao stopped the tape. He'd liked these musings about women even more than the stuff about motorcycles and racing. The topic interested him.

He began to think a bit about himself, his own life. He had imagined himself asking, "Giacomo, have you ever really loved a woman?". He hadn't asked him, though, nor would he as he was convinced the answer would have been “I loved them all”. Which, in part, was true probably true: in his way, the Winner *had* loved them all. But could it be said that he had ever been in love? That he had ever cried, really cried, for a woman? The answer, Nao, reasoned, was no. He realised it wasn’t very nice of him to be doing this solo question-and-answer routine, but he did feel sure about one thing: the Winner’s egoism had shielded him from serious pain, humiliation, suffering, the real suffering of a love that comes to an end. The Winner was hard, always had been, and this had stopped him from suffering.

Nao himself had never cried for a woman. And, at that moment, thought he never would. It just wasn’t worth the effort, he reasoned. He knew of course, that this was claptrap, just a mind game designed to shield him from thoughts that would force him to look at the harsh reality. Now in his thirties, Nao was all alone, as lonely as can be, a misfit whose only real pleasure was cruising the city by night in his car to see what happened and chat with whoever he ran into. Yet the worst thing was that he was totally unprepared to establish a mature relationship with a woman.

The women he frequented were the night-time sort. He didn’t have a girlfriend. There was a girl in his town who he chased after, but he did so without any conviction: if she’d had said she had met someone else and was going to marry him Nao would almost have felt relieved. He badgered her and called her but never concluded anything, because in truth he didn’t want to: he wasn’t ready, hadn’t thought about it, didn’t really want it. The future wasn’t something he really thought about, more out of laziness than anything else. Things, he reasoned, would be fine; he’d be able to live on for a few more years like this, on the edge of reality, until he decided to turn over a new leaf, get married and start a family. It all looked very simple.

In the meantime he continued to stay in his micro-home, where no-one - especially women - ever visited. The ones he did meet – who charged for their company – were encountered in cars or one-star hotels. He hadn’t even begun to search for a female companion, someone to marry. After all, he liked the bachelor lifestyle. One day he’d start looking, and was sure he would find someone too. That was when he’d sell his flat and buy a bigger place with her, set up a family nest. She would, mind you, have to pay for her half of the house.

Nao stood up, stretched, checked his mobile for messages (not that there were ever any messages other than those associated with work, so no-one ever texted him at this time) and took a stroll around the room. Then he sat back down and let the tape play on.

NAO How much is left of that boy who dreamed of racing, who wanted to become a champion, when he succeeds and crowns his dreams? Is there a part of him that remains child-like? What changes?

GIACOMO Whether you race motorcycles or not, change is something you can always count on. Personally, I don't *feel* any different, I always feel the same. Yesterday a professor who had been my teacher, and is now eighty-three years old, said that he'd written about me, my naturalness, importance, sacrifices and honesty towards the world. To be truthful, I wasn't aware I'd become so important to the world! When I look at the others, Valentino Rossi for example, I think, "He's so important!". It's only now that I realise I'm the only person, perhaps, who has achieved more than him. He's still young, and will go on to do much more: but at the moment I'm still in the lead. Yet for a very long time I was stuck in my shell. I never said, "Now I'm World Champion and can do whatever I like". I used to go to Lovere to see my parents, hang out around the lake. I mean, I changed in many ways because I'd become someone, because I'd won – no, *dominated* – not only the Italian championship but also the World Championship, and won it fifteen times: but deep down, *inside*, I've hardly changed at all. Being a winner had a dream-like quality to it. I thought, "What? Me, a guy from Lovere? Me who dreamt of racing and am now beating everyone…". But at the time I didn't give it too much thought. Then, as I got older, I looked back on what I'd done and realised the magnitude of it. I used to get invited everywhere and meet celebrities of every kind. I've met Gianni Agnelli, Enzo Ferrari, the President of the Republic, Prince Phillip, who gave me a congratulatory slap on the back at the TT. Yet I was so focussed on the racing that I didn't think these things exceptional. Now I can see that they were.

NAO Is there still a bit of the child left in you?

GIACOMO There are the memories of childhood.

NAO Were you more altruist as a child or was there already that element of selfishness that came out in the racing?

GIACOMO I was pretty normal I reckon, the way I am now: I give if I get. I don't want to be the one doing the thanking all the time. I want to get thanked as well. I can't keep giving without getting. Just as it's not right to get without giving. Maybe we'd all like to receive lots without having to put out, but there has to be a balance.

NAO So: as a kid you gave more than you got, then later on you instinctively switched to a more demanding mindset?

GIACOMO Oh, no, I wasn't a giver. I mean, I gave what it was right to, or perhaps tried to remain one up in the give-and-take stakes. You live and learn: you meet all these people but it's so hard to figure out who the good guys are – there are always so few of them. So you become more cautious about everything, and that includes giving, because there might come a point when you receive nothing more in return. People don't give a shit sometimes: you'll lend something and get it back broken, ruined, because they didn't look after it or, rather, didn't look after it the way you would have done. I'd be happy to lend my bike, but I already know it's going to be treated carelessly, that they won't change gear when they should, that they'll fry the brakes. It's so annoying to get stuff back and find it's been treated thoughtlessly. For instance, I hate it when you go skiing and at the end of the day the others get in the car with their ski boots covered in snow and ice. It drives me nuts! I mean, is it so hard to wipe them off before you get in? Like I said, most people don't give a damn. Another thing: I always take my shoes off when I come in, and I'd never wear them on the carpets. That was a habit I picked up in Japan. Well, to tell the truth I already had the habit, which might be why I got on so well with the people there. They were incredibly respectful, polite and clean. Instead, when my friends came to Japan they'd snigger when they had to take their shoes off in the restaurant.

NAO Did you have any recurring dreams during the week leading up to the race or the night before it?

GIACOMO All the dreams were the same: I was racing, would fly up in the air and crash. Then I'd be awake, sweating and frightened. I had that dream many times. Other riders had similar dreams. I also used to dream of falling into a ravine during the race.

NAO Why do you think you dreamt these things? Was it out of fear, the deep-down awareness that what you were doing was perilous?

GIACOMO When they used to say to us, "You're crazy, foolhardy, you don't realise what you're risking", I'd reply "No, that's not true, we do it out of passion". We felt that passion, just as we *knew* of the dangers. I knew I could die. For instance, I'd go to the Tourist Trophy, my mother would fret her heart out and implore me – can you imagine - to "Go slowly": sometimes I'd have to look the other way when I said goodbye because, knowing there was a good chance of dying, the tears would well up in my eyes. Because back then we did die. I lost a lot of friends. It could happen to me or anyone else. When Kato died in 2003 it had been ten years since the last fatality. In my day we'd die at the rate of five or six a *year*. I don't know if I'd call it fear, it was more a sharp awareness of how things were, the reality of it. Not that it made us slow up: you raced, strove to win and put all such thoughts from your mind. Yet when the race was over you sometimes thought, "Jesus, that was so close! I nearly killed myself!". Or someone would come up to you and say "So-and-so is dead", and you'd think, "How come it always happens to the others?". Unlike today, this was the saddest side of things. Like at Monza, when Pasolini and Saarinen died: it could so easily have been me. Because when you went into the bend at 250 kph and were hemmed in by walls or guardrails and you came off – not necessarily out of any fault of yours but perhaps because the engine had seized, the chain had broken, a tyre had burst, you'd hit a patch of oil – you were as good as dead. It didn't matter how skilled you were. When you're good, sure, you think it's never going to happen: but it did, and to the best too.

NAO Were there times when you thought: "Yes, yes, it can happen to me too – but it never will".

GIACOMO It's a mechanism we all employ, all the time. It's certainly not confined to racing. Remember that plane that went down in Egypt a short time ago, the one heading for Sharm El Sheik I think it was? My friend was there when it happened, swimming in the Red Sea. And then he comes back and proposes we get back out there for Easter, the logic being that it's only just happened and another crash is hardly likely to happen again on the same route straight away is it? Wherever there's risk we play mind games to steel ourselves: and that's what I used to do when I raced.

NAO So you're saying that nightmares bring to the surface thoughts we bury with logic. Is that it?

GIACOMO Might be, seeing as other riders said they had the same sort of dreams.

NAO Who?

GIACOMO Nieto, and Pasolini I believe.

NAO So it's as if a hidden part of you says "Look, this is how things stand, you know it... You do understand what's at stake here, don't you?". But it's only said through dreams, because a rider will never openly declare it to himself. His conscious self will say "It'll never happen to me".

GIACOMO Exactly.

NAO Can we speak about Count Agusta, the tyrant owner of MV?

GIACOMO MV had got hold of Carlo Ubbiali on the phone at Bergamo and he'd given them my number. Magni called me at home in Lovere, where I was still living, and told me that Count Agusta wanted to see me. I nearly fainted when he said that. I was given an appointment at five in the afternoon, but I was there at half-four. I parked and the secretary accompanied me to the waiting room. Five o'clock came and went. Every now and again Magni would pass by and ask if the Count had called me in yet. I waited and waited: six o'-clock came and went, as did seven o'clock. I told the secretary that I hadn't eaten since midday and that it was getting on for eight. She said the Count was a busy man: which with all those comings and goings around his office door, was undoubtedly the case. "Just sit tight", she said. I felt like getting up and going a few times but said to myself, "I get an appointment with Count Agusta and then *leave*?". It was 10 pm when I was called in. Magni was there too. I went into this rather shadowy room and the Count was sat down, bent over his desk, which was on a sort of raised dais. As I walked towards him he raised his head and said: "Who are you?" he barked. I felt awful, I was terrified. "I'm Agostini". I said. "And what do you want?". What on earth does he mean, I thought. I've been waiting here for five hours and now he asks me what I want, when it was *him* that called *me*... I just replied flatly, "I want to race your motorcycles". And him: "Are you good enough for my motorcycles?". Again I was baffled by his behaviour. So I said: "Try me". How on earth I got that out, being so introverted, I'll never know... "All right", he replied. Then he turned to Magni and said, "Right, Arturo, tomorrow take him to Monza and try him out. Lay out the cones and see how he gets on, then report back". All this with Magni and I standing in front of his desk. We left and I said to Magni, "What a strange fellow this Count is. First he chases me up then he asks me what I want". And Magni: "Forget it, that's how he is". "Yeah, right, but are you telling me that I, the Italian Champion, have to go to Monza to ride around some *cones*?". "It's of no importance: just shut up and do as he said". I went home and told my father what had happened. "It doesn't matter", he said, "it obviously wasn't the right moment. Relax". The next day, at Monza, they'd laid the cones out on the straight. It was like a throwback to my obstacle race days, so I couldn't help laughing. So I did this section of straight, up and down around the cones, just as the Count had ordered. It wasn't like today, not like Valentino Rossi and Honda who fight it out down to the last letter of the contract. Back then you were either in or you were out – and out for good. After the test the Count's secretary and the accountant, Bertolini, who saw to everything, drew up an agreement and showed it to me. I signed it hardly without reading and didn't request any changes. I didn't meet the Count again until the signing. That was in late '64. So that's how we began. He was always serious, always aloof, but I knew he liked me. At Cascina Costa I was the only one who got to park my car more or less where he did. Perhaps because one day I drove it in by mistake. Nobody had said anything: the security staff probably thought the Count had authorised me to do so, but he hadn't. In the meantime it became obvious that I got on with him: in the end my car ended up next to his. And they were the only two cars allowed there.

NAO What sort of car did you have then?

GIACOMO A Porsche 356 Super 90, the old cream-coloured type. I treated myself well.

NAO How was life at MV?

GIACOMO Whenever I was down I'd hop in the car and drive to Gallarate, the Cascina Costa racing division. It was a life-saver. If I had a headache it would pass while I was there. If I arrived down in the dumps I'd leave in high spirits. When I was there I'd check things out and tinker with the bikes. One day, towards three-thirty in the afternoon, I was watching the mechanics at work when they suddenly stood to attention. The door opened and in walked the Count. Everyone began reciting "*Buongiorno, signor conte*". That was how they called him, Signor conte - and so did I. He'd reply with a short, gruff "*Buongiorno*!". Outside a chauffeur was waiting for him in a Cadillac cabriolet. When he saw me he barked "What are you doing here?. "I'm here to look at the bikes, to see how the work is…". And him, shouting: "Out. Out of here now!" I didn't say a word: I was as in awe of him as much as anyone else. I left with a lump in my throat, his words had really upset me. "I come all the way from Lovere", I thought, "to see how things are going and instead of saying 'Well done, it's good to see you here rather than out messing about', he starts yelling at me". I felt so insulted that I really felt like slamming the door on MV there and then. I was walking back to the car when his Cadillac drew up next to me. *Signor conte* had wound the window down. As usual, a blanket covered his legs. "Where are you off to now?", he asked. "I'm going home". He could see my eyes welling up with tears and said, "Oh, come on now, you go back and check out your things, what are you going to do at home anyway?". He'd changed his mind. He could, I suppose, have been, been trying to be funny beforehand – but humour wasn't exactly his strong point. No, he needed to keep his reputation as a hard man intact, and so acted accordingly. But deep down I don't think he was so hard. In any case, I walked back to the department and that was, I think, the only real scrape I had with Count Domenico.

NAO What were the other Agustas like?

GIACOMO I remember his brother, Count Mario. He'd had the same trusted driver, Marchisio, for over twenty years. Marchisio, who was a friend, knew I'd be asking for more money when my contract came up for renewal and said so to Count Mario. When I went to see Count Mario myself he said: "When you see Micuzzo, just do what he tells you, sign what he wants, don't say anything, don't get him riled… and I'll give you the rest". Nevertheless, I still went to see Count Domenico (known to his family as Micuzzo) and asked for the rise. Then I told Count Mario I wasn't happy so he'd top things up. Count Mario was both kind and generous. "If you win this year", he once said, "I'll let you have my Ferrari 275 GTB". But before the season was over he died suddenly and unexpectedly, and after that I never asked anything else of anyone.

NAO What sort of people were the Agustas?

GIACOMO Count Mario was more open, easier-going. Count Domenico was sterner, short on smiles. He made everyone uneasy. Everyone was on edge around him: managers, engineers, mechanics… even his brothers. But don't get me wrong: they all held him in the highest esteem. One day Mazza, the mechanic, was testing an engine when in walked the count, shouting "Stop, stop! Can't you see that engine's no good?". They opened it up and the springs on one of the valves had gone. I reckon it was just a coincidence, though. Mind you, there was a similar situation with the helicopters once: they were trying out the 109 and he barked "Stop, land it now. We've got to modify a few things". The changes were made and afterwards the helicopter did, in fact, fly better.

NAO Was he lucky… or a natural born winner?

GIACOMO Who knows? But he'd hit the mark every time. For example, you couldn't change the contract one iota: either you accepted it as it was or you were out the door.

NAO Was he like that with everyone, Italians and foreigners?

GIACOMO Yes.

NAO What did he think of the riders?

GIACOMO Well, it wasn't like with *commendatore* Morini, who you'd feel at home with, have supper with. In ten years, I must have eaten with Count Domenico just three times, and always in a very formal setting. After he died Corrado took things up: he was a different kettle of fish and would invite me out on his boat. Domenico was a hard worker. He'd arrive at the office at eleven. He'd stop for lunch at two, come back at four-thirty and then carry on 'til 11 pm. Being Sicilian, he ran on Southern Italian Time. His villa was just outside the plant, which made things easier for him: he'd eat and have a nap there. Then at eleven in the evening they'd drive him back to his home in Milan.

NAO So what do you think the riders meant to him?

GIACOMO I believe he saw us as employees. He gave you a bike, your job was to win: end of story. He wasn't heartless though: at Christmas he'd turn up at the racing department with a big cardboard box containing envelopes that he'd distribute to the most deserving. There was no envelope, however, for anyone who'd screwed up, and there was always at least one: they'd get in line and wish *signor conte* season's greetings, only to receive the same in return. For them there was no bonus. Although we were never close and he never once invited me to his home, I got on well with him, perhaps because I had no pretension about becoming his friend.

NAO How was *commendatore* Morini, instead?

GIACOMO Bologna born and bred, he was more affable, cordial, friendly. We'd eat out together and he'd tell me to eat well, sleep well and stay in good hotels because it was important to treat yourself right. "Take it easy, but win" was his motto.

NAO Corrado Agusta, instead?

GIACOMO He lived his life with gusto. I'd go and see him at St. Moritz and if I wanted to do some skiing he'd give me a lift to the top of the mountain in his helicopter: then I'd ski back down. Not that the rest of the family lived like paupers. They all had their boats, for example, and when they docked at Capri the people practically got on their knees to beg for a job because they used to give tips of 10 or 15 thousand lira, often for doing next to nothing. Once Mario and Domenico hosted me on their boat in Capri, and I was flabbergasted at just how servile people were to them. Then I saw the tips they were giving and realised why. Another time at Capri I was staying at the hotel Quisisana and had an appointment with Count Domenico to discuss the racing. I turned up at eleven in the morning, as agreed but he was late as usual. Presently I heard a woman bawling "Bastard of a f***ing Count!". I could see the count coming towards, with his wife, a minute woman barely one metre twenty tall, following close behind and hurling abuse at him, right there in the hall of the Quisisana... "This man has five thousand employees", I thought, "who all tremble and kow-tow when they see him, yet he lets himself be treated like this by such a tiny woman". The count saw me and said, "Come on, let her get on with her shouting. She's in a bit of a mood". The scene made a lasting impression on me.

NAO Was the Count a racing fan?

GIACOMO Yes. It wasn't just a business to him, he could be quite passionate about it. In my day he didn't attend as many races, he'd only come to the GP races every now and then; he was, after all, getting on a bit. Before though, in the early 60s, he would never fail to show up at the season's inauguration in Modena. Magni told me that his mother and brother - the whole family - would show up. They even used to amuse themselves by each promising a different rider money if he won: it was a way of sharpening their competitiveness. Towards the late sixties the empire that had been built by Count Domenico started requiring a lot of attention and he no longer had the time or energy to see all the races.

NAO Did he ever call you to discuss the races? Did he say what he wanted?

GIACOMO Yes, in his matter-of-fact way. He'd just ask me how things were going, why I'd done things this way or why he thought it would have been better if I'd done them that way. There was no dialogue as such. He'd sometimes ask you a question and then say "That's all, thank you", without even waiting for the answer. All said and done, you were one of his employees.

NAO Did that bother you?

GIACOMO No. As long as they gave me a winning motorcycle, I couldn't really have cared less. Well, friendlier relations would have been more welcome but, you know, he was on a different planet: I was just this youngster, he a count with helicopters, planes, boats and what have you. Even if he just laid his hand on my shoulder it seemed out of place. I almost felt like thanking him for those small gestures of fondness.

NAO What changed after Domenico's death?

Tourist Trophy on the Isle of Man: Giacomo flies over the hump
of the Ballaugh Bridge on his 3-cylinder MV. He would win the TT ten times.

Above: Giacomo with Gianni Agnelli at the paddocks in Monza.
Below: the walk to the start with trusted aid Angelo Conti.

As he checks the gear ratio tables, the champion bites his nails:
one of several tension-releasing habits.

One of Agostini's most respected opponents: Renzo Pasolini.
Their thrilling duels made motorcycling Emilia-Romagna's most popular sport.

Late sixties: motorhomes were still a thing of the future and a motorcycle transport van was sometimes the only MV racing department vehicle to be seen at the race venue.

Assen, Holland. Agostini (MV) and Mike Hailwood (Honda) battle for supremacy in the 500 class. Hailwood, perhaps his toughest opponent, was also renowned for his fair play.

Above: Hailwood hugs Agostini. Below: Giacomo with Count Domenico Agusta (right) and his nephew Rocky, who would later become MV team manager.

Giacomo Agostini on the three-cylinder MV 350 on the Hockenheim circuit (Germany): as always, riding in the wet narrowed the safety margin considerably.

The Seventies. Despite having won the World Championship several times, Agostini gets little privacy as he suits up in the midst of fans. Motorhomes and their comforts are still a long way off.

Above: at the Bar Moderno, in Lovere, where Monday evenings would see Agostini give friends the race rundown. Below: the champion smiles for photographers at the insidious Sachensring.

Everybody loves a winner: here Agostini reels off the autographs for his growing pool of fans.

In Great Britain safety was the least of anyone's worries, especially the public's.
Below: Agostini enjoys a hunting trip.

On the Cesenatico straight at full speed: Agostini flies over a rise as he hunkers down behind the windshield to optimise aerodynamics.

Tourist Trophy 1967: the chain on Agostini's MV snaps as he leads on the last lap, a full eight seconds ahead of Mike Hailwood (Honda).

Winner takes all: Agostini went for the best in cars too. Here he poses next to one of his first Porsches, a yellow 912.

Leader of the pack: at the Ospedaletti circuit (Imperia) Agostini leads this 1971 race on his beloved three-cylinder MV 500.

GIACOMO Quite a few things really, because he had been the playmaker, the driving force. For instance, he had wanted the three-cylinder engine. He was the one who wanted to get involved in racing, the one who knew about it too. After his death, in 1971, things slowly altered. Then Mario died and Corrado, left on his own, slowly relinquished his grip on it and it was all over.

NAO Was it Count Domenico who wanted an Italian rider for the MV Agusta?

GIACOMO Yes, he wanted an Italian on his new three-cylinder. With Morini I had been clocking up the victories. So Arturo Magni and Ubbiali told him I might be the champion he'd been looking for. With Morini we used to test on a long straight in Bologna, where even the police would turn out to enjoy the show. I'd already told *commendatore* Morini that I'd be leaving, seeing as the contract was about to expire. Now, he always used to get to the office between eleven and twelve, but that day he was down on the test straight at half past nine, asking "So, what are your plans?". And me: "*Commendatore*, you know how it is...". "No, no. I've got the contract here. You just write the figure you want and stay with me". Since I'd started out with them, first with the 175 then the 250, and because he'd put so much trust in me, it was all quite sad. In my heart, I didn't want to go, because I'd been looked after extremely well and I knew he was fond of me. "*Commendatore*" I said, "you don't compete in the World Championships, but MV do. They've got the 350, the 500, the *classe regina*...". "No, no, you sign here, keep on winning and we'll soon have something in the World Championships too...". "To be honest", I went on, "I have to think of my career, I need to move on, do the World Championships". He was upset about it but understood and let me go, even though with Morini I was winning everything. He realised my destiny lay in the big-cylinder bikes, and that, in fact, is how it turned out.

NAO So being a champion is all about making the right choices?

GIACOMO Yes, but not just that. As I said, you need God-given talent but you need to work on it, develop it, know how to handle things. If you've got talent you need to blend it with intelligence so you can see the way forward and figure out how far you can go. There were plenty of other good riders back then but few knew how to handle themselves or work hard. It takes sacrifice, preparation... For example, towards the end of '64, when Gilera were offering me twice as much, I signed up with MV because my father had advised me to stick with the bigger company, where the technology was. I'd resisted the immediate temptation of the money and had, instead, looked ahead and made the right choice: I went on to win thirteen world titles with MV. If I'd gone with Gilera (who didn't have much success) things may well have gone very differently for me. I'd probably have missed the train altogether.

NAO The mid-sixties was a bad time for Italian motorcycling, and only MV were competing at the highest levels.

GIACOMO Yes, things had started out well enough with MV, Benelli and Gilera. The latter had given bikes to Derek Minter and Geoff Duke, who self-managed them. Then Honda and MZ, came along, then Honda left, then in stepped Yamaha: they'd made a 4-cylinder 250 that went faster than my 500! At Hockenheim there was half a second per lap between the Yamaha 250 and the MV 500, in my favour: but I had twice the cylinder capacity! However, Yamaha's engines were fragile and broke down frequently and the motorcycle wasn't easy to handle. It had tons of power, so much that the technicians had to weight the fork down, otherwise it was always up in the air: it was an astonishing bike.

NAO What happened to the Italian constructors in the mid-sixties?

GIACOMO The Italians were swept away by the Japanese: Yamaha, Honda, Suzuki, Kawasaki.

NAO How do you choose a competition bike: for power, handling, suspension set-up?

GIACOMO It's the whole package that counts. Because if you've got the power but not the handling then you're never going to be able to make the most of the horsepower so it's as if you don't have it. A bike that handles superbly but is short on power is the same thing. A good motorcycle is a good compromise: you need the power *and* the handling. The MV was a great bike because, most of all, I was picky: I wanted everything on the bike perfect, the brakes, the clutch, the tyres, the wheels, the frame, the engine. It was this blend that made the MV a winner, despite having only a little more HP than the Benelli; on some occasions, it had a bit less too, but the point is that nothing was left to chance. Don't get me wrong, I don't want to boast, it's just that I *was* a perfectionist and I always kept a close eye on everything bike-wise. A great-looking bike wasn't enough for me: I would go down to the racing department, check everything; I'd pick up the shock absorber and take it to Ceriani to have it inspected. Hailwood, for instance, did none of this. And he'd still win, 'cause he didn't need to do it. Yet technical problems tended to penalise him more than they did me, and you can imagine why. For example, there was this one race when I was with MV, at Abbazia in Yugoslavia. I was up against a Yamaha that had an engine weighing just thirty-five kilograms against my hefty sixty. I had the mechanics set up an extremely tight first gear, so tight that they initially refused to fit it. I insisted: "Do it this way". "No", they replied, "you can't have a first gear that tight because when you put it in second you'll skip 50 kph and the engine revs will drop like a stone". Luckily, they went along with me and at every hairpin in the race, I gained a second: I'd come out of the bend, accelerate, gain some ground, then lose a little when the engine sputtered after the change into second: but the gains outweighed the losses, vindicating the choice. Three seconds gained here and two lost there still make a one-second gain. Even the mechanics who'd disagreed, because they'd never really considered it as an option, were won over when they saw the results. The stopwatch states facts, not opinions.

NAO Describe what happened when you broke away from the Agustas at the end of 1973.

GIACOMO The decision to leave the Agustas and sign up with Yamaha was a difficult one. It was like leaving a family. I'd been with them thirteen years, had won everything. Yet I could see the 4-stroke era was at an end and that the future lay in 2-strokes. I was right, because just two years later the 4-strokes had gone and the 2-strokes remained the norm for the following twenty years. Yamaha had already sounded me out two years previously and I'd said no, because I knew their engines had a tendency to seize. Yet over those two years they had made considerable progress and their 2-strokes were better by then. So Yamaha offered me an opportunity, and just as I'd done when I was with Morini, I looked ahead and took it. I knew that there was no 2-stroke project at MV and I knew that I'd have to change if I wanted to keep on winning. It cost me dearly: I had to build up a whole new "family", in Japan, a far-away land where things are done differently. But I was focussed on my career, so I decided it had to be done. I wrote a thank-you letter to the Count, explaining my regret. They were pretty unhappy about it all at first, but in the end they understood that it was a step I needed to take. In any case, MV wanted to demonstrate they could win without me, just as Honda did with Valentino.

NAO How did you find Japan?

GIACOMO I loved it immediately. The people were lovely, and if I wanted anything it was given immediately. My first stay there lasted fifteen days. I'd turn up at the track at nine-thirty, ten at the latest, and stop testing at about half-twelve. Then I'd test some more from two to four. They'd take me back to the hotel and then out to dinner: I wasn't left alone for a moment, I always had company. When I asked where I could buy some bread, because I was getting tired of eating rice all the time, the driver started taking me to the baker's to get a baguette each day. Everyone would laugh as I approached the track with the baguette tucked under my arm. In just three or four days I had the two-stroke engine figured and things proceeded smoothly. However, for Daytona we'd only tested the 500 and the 700, but not the 350. I only got to try it out hurriedly, just before leaving: but I left instructions – the front fork had to be a certain length, a certain angle and so on. I also asked them to modify the frame. A month later they informed me that they'd made all the changes I'd requested and that their test rider had shaved two seconds off his lap times. I was delighted and I think it helped boost my stock with the Japanese too. However, that first year I fell in Sweden and broke my shoulder: Barry Sheene had fallen in front of me and I ploughed into him. I had to skip four World Championship races. Of course, it pissed me off that MV had demonstrated they could win without me, seeing as Read has swept to victory. But I was laid up in hospital, so there wasn't much I could do about it. Nevertheless, I won the 350 title and the following year took the World Championship in the 500.

NAO How did the first contacts with Yamaha come about?

GIACOMO Two years earlier Yamaha's managing director, Mr. Hasegawa - who later became company chairman and held the position until just two years ago - came to Lovere. I turned him down because their motorbikes still weren't reliable enough and I was also worried about falling. Two years later I saw they'd made progress, and when Rod Gould got in touch and pushed a contract in front of me, saying "You write the figure", I knew I was ready, mature: I wrote the figure and that was that.

NAO What do you mean, "You write the figure?".

GIACOMO Since they want to whisk you away from the manufacturer you're already working with they know there's no point in bargaining, and when you tell them what you want they're generally happy to oblige. It's not that I asked for a ridiculous amount: I wasn't stupid, I knew what the limits were. So when the OK came through from Japan, I signed.

NAO Without stating figures, is it true that you made excellent money? And would you also agree that you were the only one doing so on the World Championship circuit back then?

GIACOMO Yes. I was N°1. I won everything. When I went to Yamaha I'd already won thirteen world titles. They were aware – everyone was – that I knew what I wanted and hardly ever made mistakes. They knew what they were getting: they wanted a technician who would help them develop their bikes. In two years I won two titles. And if I hadn't fallen in Sweden – which wasn't my fault anyway – it would have been three.

NAO Did you ever have any trouble adapting to Japan?

GIACOMO At first I was a bit lost, but I was also excited to be discovering so many new things, their way of life… One evening the chairman of Yamaha, Mr. Eguchi, organised a raw fish dinner in my honour at one of Hamamatsu's finest restaurants: unfortunately I just couldn't eat it, nor pretend to do so. It was just so embarrassing: they were all so proud to have taken me to this famous restaurant, only to see me spitting out gobs of fish… They were quite nice about it though. There were always two minders with me. I had nothing of my own, not even a wallet: all I had to do was express a desire for something and it would materialise as if by magic. Every evening they'd take me along to the discotheque where the geishas would cheer things up. A geisha is no prostitute: she's a feel-good professional who only goes so far and no further. She'll put you at ease, take off your shoes, put them back on, wipe your mouth as you eat, keep your glass filled, wash your hands, amuse you, light your cigarette, all as if it were a game and no more. Many are wives with families and are simply career geishas.

NAO Do you see Japanese women as being at the service of the men.

GIACOMO Once, a Yamaha manager invited me to his house: there were six of us and his wife never actually sat down at the table herself. She served us, she removed everyone's shoes – and yet she was the wife of one of the most powerful managers. On the whole I liked Japan, perhaps also out of an enthusiasm for a country that was so different from mine, the discovery of new customs and habits. For example, they'd eat cross-legged on the floor, which was extraordinary to me. I remember that meat cost a fortune – perhaps 250 Euros a kilo. Now it's twice as much, perhaps more. The meat from cows that were massaged, that drank beer not water. The cost of living was astronomical: I remember being in awe of the figures. I got special treatment, of course, but I think I would have liked it just as much even without that. That's probably why I still enjoy good relations with Yamaha, and if I need anything I just call and they come running. I'm still close friends with the managers I knew back then who are still with the company.

The tape ended.

Nao was happy with the questions he'd asked so far: he still liked them now, some months after he'd asked them.

The most striking thing about the tape was, considered Nao, the coldness with which Agostini had made all the choices, behaving rather like a bee, flitting from one pollen-filled flower to the next, juicier one so as to maximise his own payback and build his career. There can't be too much sentiment in the workplace, thought Nao. That was the same for everyone, sportsmen and journalists alike. A rider who becomes a champion has almost certainly been more ungrateful and selfish than all the others.

Selfishness is one of life's key concepts. It can mean success and even survival. It's egoism that allows us to love: we can only make other people happy when we're feeling good about ourselves. And we're only too glad to make them happy, because when they are, we are. Loving someone doesn't mean giving yourself to them. It means making them happy. They're two different things. Making a person happy, knew Nao, took hard work, reasoning, the application of a little trickery and underhandedness. Certainly not instinct or madness!

His thoughts went back to a Saturday afternoon on which he'd gone along with Agostini to watch his son play football. He'd called his son over, said hello, given him a few words of encouragement before leaving almost immediately. All told, they couldn't have been there more than five minutes. "We've put in our appearance", Agostini had said, "and Giacomino will be glad". Nao remembered thinking that this little vignette had made Agostini seem even shrewder: he had known that the important thing was to go along. The fact that it was only five minutes counted little.

After listening to the tape, it occurred to him that Agostini's words conveyed more of what it meant to be a winner than he'd originally noticed. His first impression had been that the Winner's answers were a little banal, but on re-listening to the tape he realised that his words contained not only truth but also sentiment. Whenever he illustrated anything he did so through plain narrative, without emotion or involvement. He laid out the actions, the facts – but now Nao had begun to read between the lines and perceive the thoughts and feelings behind them. All this, thought Nao, was a good thing: Agostini, in a sense, would end up explaining himself. He went to bed, unperturbed and encouraged.

Tape n° 3
The need to hate your rival

The next morning Nao was brushing his teeth in front of the IKEA-framed mirror, gazing blankly into his own eyes. He was thinking.

As he'd slept Agostini's words had meandered through his mind. Without quite realising why, he'd remembered that he'd called his daughter Vittoria, his son Piergiacomo (known as Giacomino, or Giac) - and the dog Ago. His entire world was right there in those names, wrapped around the legend of the rider who'd won more than anyone else in the entire history of motorcycling. *Fifteen* world titles: an enormity. Yet does, Nao asked himself, becoming a legend mean becoming a slave to that legend?

As he thought all this he began to feel better than he had a few minutes before. Yes, whenever, he came up with intelligent thoughts (and he often did), he would smile, the glow of self-satisfaction spreading across his face.

In the wake of these last thoughts he remembered what Agostini had told him about how he'd come to choose his daughter's name. At first he hadn't known what to call her – the right name just kept eluding him. Then, a former racer, Nico Cereghini, during a break at one the GPs Agostini had attended just to stay in touch with the racing world, had said "Eh, Mino, having a kid is just one more victory (*vittoria*, in Italian) for a guy like you". At this Agostini's eyes nearly popped out of his head. "Of course", he'd blurted, "the name's been staring me in the face and I never realised it: my daughter is the last *vittoria* of my career!".

However, things hadn't gone so smoothly when it had come to choosing the title of the book. As usual, Agostini had his own ideas, but Nao hadn't been so sure they were the right ones.

Nao was certain that the right title was *L'uomo moto* (Motorcycle Man). It summed up Agostini to a tee and represented him for what he was: a man who's vocation in life was motorcycling and racing, someone who'd achieved as much in that field as *could* be achieved. It was just what the reader would look for: a staggeringly successful career in which he lived in symbiosis with the motorcycle, making him a modern day centaur, half motorcycle, half man. Nao loved that title. Yet Agostini didn't. No, he had never liked it, Nao was sure of it, probably because it made him two-dimensional by narrowing the spotlight so it only focussed on the motorcycle-rider-and-great-champion. But whether Agostini liked it or not, that is exactly what he was - just as all those trophies testified. Agostini had probably expected something more gratifying, more fawning or self-celebrating. He'd put his own ideas forward, of course. They had been so banal and obvious as to be almost unrepeatable. He was the "Number One", but there was no way that was going on the cover when Agostini himself was one of the co-authors; and in any case, that title has already been used by Hans Ruesch years before. Agostini had asked, seeing as so much time had gone by, whether it might be used anyway. Nao had skated around the argument. He'd also managed to dissuade Agostini from titles such as "Born Talented", "A life on a Motorcycle" or "Passion for Motorcycling".

As they continued to meet up for interviews, another biography on Agostini, written by a British journalist, had come out. Ago had gone wild because no-one had told him anything about it and because it was packed with errors and inaccuracies. The only thing he'd liked about it had been the title. It was "Champion of Champions".

Nao had tried everything to convince Agostini that Motorcycle Man was the right title for his book, but Agostini had stonewalled. Once, as Nao brought up the matter for the umpteenth time, the Winner's patience had evaporated. "No! For the last time, no!", he'd shouted. "I've asked everyone and no-one likes it. I'm not presumptuous like some people, you know. I know enough to listen to other people's opinions too, and the fact is that I can't find anyone who likes *L'uomo moto*!".

That was the last time they talked about it. Nao had said, "Very well, Giacomo, you decide on the title". And his reply had been a simple "Okay". A couple of weeks later, with the kind of voice employed by those who won't be contradicted, Agostini had called him and said, "I've got a title: 'Fifteen times'. Every time I speak in public, that's how I get presented. That's the title for our book".

"Giacomo, it's just perfect", Nao had said.

That evening, after work and the usual bland bachelor supper, Nao promptly started re-running the tapes.

NAO Why did you stop racing?

GIACOMO A few races had gone badly. At Mugello my Yamaha 350 seized on the last lap, something that *never happens*. An engine seizure might happen at the start of the race, but not the end. I fell and broke my shoulder: that was my last race. Not only that, it was the first race in which my brother Felice had been in front of me, and I wasn't feeling aggressive enough to overtake him, I was afraid he might take too many risks to keep pace with me. It was a season where just too many things were going wide of the mark, and since I was used to things being on beam, I started wondering why. I began thinking that maybe something or someone was trying to tell me that I'd already got a heck of a lot out of motorcycling and that now was the time to bring things to a close, to stop being selfish, to be happy with my lot. So I retired.

NAO So the signs were there. What year was it?

GIACOMO It was 1977. I was still winning, but there were a series of mechanical failures, odd things that had never occurred in twenty years of racing. Once, the drive shaft broke a hundred metres from the finish, another time the bike failed to start on the grid. Then there were the seizures… just too many omens. It all made me reflect. Looking back, maybe I'd just run out of gas, used up all the gifts that mother nature had been so generous with. I began to realise that I might be pushing my luck.

NAO So you hadn't decided that it would be your last year. The decision came as the season unfolded.

GIACOMO Yes. It was that last race at Mugello that clinched it. I reasoned I'd had everything, perhaps far more than I had even hoped. And the deaths of so many riders over the years had left their mark.

NAO How does a rider react to a fall? Physical injury aside, what sort of mental scars does it leave?

GIACOMO You always think you're immortal, that some things will just never happen to *you*. When *you* fall, you think of the friend who came off worse or the one who came off worse than *him*. Of course, if you do fall and are unharmed or only slightly injured then that depends not so much on your skill as on the part of your body you land on: maybe the shoulder, perhaps a leg, but never the head. And not because you're clever, but because of the luck of the draw. I've always tried to fall as little as possible. Any fall is, to an extent, a wake-up call: it makes you aware it can happen to you too and that the consequences can never really be known. In Czechoslovakia the gearbox jammed and I was thrown against a wall, but I was only doing twenty or thirty. If I'd been doing a hundred I wouldn't be here now. No fall is without consequences, not even a so-called simple one. When you're young you'll quickly forget about it, but as the years go on they leave a more lasting impression. Just look at the stir caused by Kato's death: It was years since anyone had died[1]. Did you see how it provoked worldwide discussion, how gutted everyone was, the people in tears? Imagine this happening, as it did in my day, not every eight-nine years but two or three times *every year.* Think how that made us feel.

NAO Lets try and identify the most memorable race of your career, the race of your life. Just as Muhammad Alì defined his bout with George Foreman in Kinshasa as the bout of his life...

GIACOMO There have been plenty of important races in my career. But there is one into which I put body and soul, one where I performed to the limit. Even now, I sometimes dream about. It was one of the most difficult circuits against one of the toughest opponents in the world. It was the 1967 Tourist Trophy. Hailwood had moved to Honda and I had been left to defend the MV colours by myself.

NAO So how did it go?

GIACOMO I left Lovere in my yellow Porsche 911, just seven or eight days before the race. A few days later I was joined by loads of friends who had driven or flown in. I crossed the St. Gothard and crossed France, fuelling myself on baguettes and cheese. The MV truck, which had accompanied me part of the way, had a good store of salami and wine. although that wasn't for me (I didn't drink) but the team. We'd stocked up because we knew we weren't too keen on British cooking. We then got the ferry from Calais to Dover and drove up through England to Liverpool where we got the ferry to Douglas. This ferry was practically 'motorbikes only': it was the UK's grand motorcycling fortnight. Seeing that ferry always made an impression on me: brimming with leather-jacketed passengers... it was incredible. Everyone knew me but pretended not to, because the British fans were different from their Italian and French counter-

NOTE:[1] Daijiro Kato (Japan, 1976), 250 cc World Champion in 2001, died on 19th April 2003 after falling at Suzuka. There had been no fatal accidents in the world championship since 1994.

parts: they were very discrete. They might look at you and wait for you to turn round and give an autograph, but they were never insistent. I mean, just look how the British queue up – no shoving, just patient waiting. At first I thought no-one knew me, but nothing could have been further from the truth. They all knew me quite well, but they didn't gush their excitement like we might and they didn't have the Italian's sense of reverence. They treated you as an acquaintance, not a star. Douglas amazed me just as it always had done: a town ruled by motorcyclists, where everyone could let their exhausts pipes roar as much as they liked and generally do what they wanted. For instance, when I got up at four-thirty in the morning to go to the start for qualifying, I left my hotel on the bike with the exhausts wide open. The lorry would go ahead and a car with two mechanics would wait for me: They'd give me the bike and I'd ride towards the start with the car following behind. This gave me a chance to warm up the engine up and check out the bike. I started out from Douglas Bay Hotel, riding along the long beachfront, first idling the engine then shifting into first and second... The atmosphere was electric. The hotel had a forecourt with lots of small lock-ups that looked like they'd been designed specifically with motorcycles in mind. It hosted not only our team but Yamaha and Honda as well, and each team had a number of lock-ups proportional to its size. In the morning all I did was get up, go down and pick up the bike and then ride to the start. The qualifying started at 4.45. First, everyone got in line for a cup of tea at a kiosk run by some old ladies. It was often cold and misty. Sometimes fog or drizzle would delay the start by an hour or two. The paddock area was a huge lawn, where the teams would pitch tents and try to stay warm before the off. It was a far cry from the motorhomes of today where the cook prepares a frothy cappuccino and someone else warms your leathers or cleans your helmet.

NAO How many lorries and mechanics left Cascina Costa for the Isle of Man that time?

GIACOMO I always had five mechanics at the TT, two complete 350 and 500 motorcycles plus three spare engines for the 350 and three for the 500. All this would fit onto a large lorry belonging to MV, but we'd often take two smaller lorries because the large one would sometimes be a problem on the ferry. Today there's a truck with the tents, one to set up the hospitality facility, one for electronics, one for the tyres... I had four wheels, because I had more money than anyone else. Now they get twenty each. And there were only two tyre types.

NAO Had you already raced in the TT before '67?

GIACOMO Yes, in '65 and '66. The first time I rode the route was in the summer of '65. I'd driven up and rented the motorbike from a mechanic. I'd set off at nine and come back at midday. Then I'd go back out at two and return at 4.30. On a good day I'd complete the circuit five times: that's 350 kilometres. I'd gone off on my own that time: it was a real downer. I kept thinking of my friends, enjoying themselves back at the bar… Sometimes, when it all got to be a bit too much, I'd go and see this guy I'd met who'd married an Italian. They'd cook some spaghetti up for me. I'd squirt on some ketchup and break an egg into it to make it look like *spaghetti alla carbonara*. I was in bed by ten-thirty. I was there twelve days, and there was no mobile phone to keep you company back then. To make a call I had to go through the switchboard: they'd put you on hold for ages… But I toughed it out because I wanted to achieve the goal I'd set myself: to learn as much about the circuit as possible. Now, you can go to Misano, go whenever you like, and in a day do seventy or eighty laps. There, it would take you a fortnight to do seventy laps. And it takes 150-180 laps to learn a circuit properly. At Jerez, for instance, you can do seventy laps a day and so you can suss things out in just three days. At the TT, it would take three years to do 180 laps, so there was no way you'd figure things out in less than two years. The first year I raced, in fact, I got overtaken by Phil Read on a downhill S-bend: was in fourth gear and really moving. I couldn't believe my eyes: I'd left ten seconds ahead of him and just half-way round the circuit he'd caught me. Downhill, me in fourth, him in fifth. How come? Because on the first lap I had to try it in third, then on the second lap in third again with another 500 revs, then in fourth and so on; but it took 30 minutes to do a lap, so improving your performance on any one bend meant another three laps. Until I'd learnt it well there was no way I could start pushing it. At Ballaugh Bridge, for instance, you had to do the jump three times to figure out whether it could be taken at a certain speed or not, if everything was working smoothly. That meant another 180 km. That was why the TT would take its toll on the young: they'd think they knew it but it was almost impossible to know it all by heart and go at full throttle everywhere. For instance, Parlotti died where there were three very similar bends, one of which needed to be taken with 1000 revs less. He went into it with just 500 revs less, couldn't keep the bike on the road and plunged into a ravine. It was such a complex circuit that I had a book where I jotted everything down: the gears, the revs, the braking points... There was a saying: if you win the TT, you're already world champion. Instead, if you won the world championship, it might not be because you were so hot but simply because you got lucky, because a rival fell or another withdrew. I'd have to agree with that. Mario Lega said pretty much the same thing: "Yes, I thought Agostini was good, but not incredibly so. Then, when I saw the TT and learnt that he'd won it *ten times* I changed my mind, He was *really* good". For us riders the TT was a crucial event, because we all knew it was the hardest race in the world, and if you won it you had class.

NAO How did they establish the starting order?

GIACOMO The first were assigned by draw. The best riders started off in front, but just because you had the number one it didn't mean you would start off first.

NAO In 1965 you came third behind Redman and Read in the 350 and in the 500 you fell when you were behind Hailwood. In 1966 you won in the 350 and came second in the 500 behind Hailwood. In 1967 you came second in the 350 and in the 500 you withdrew. Which of these last two was "the race"?

GIACOMO The 500, an astonishing race. I went off first, Hailwood ten seconds afterwards. We battled it out without ever setting eyes on each other. I had mechanics scattered around the course and they would tell me how things were going by holding up a blackboard with a number indicating the gap with a plus or minus sign. We never drew near each other: I'd have the upper hand at one check point, Hailwood would be ahead at the next. I'd go like lightning as fast as Ramsey, then he'd claw back quite a lot of time up through the hills to the high points. On the downhill section, back to the start, we were more or less level. So I'd gain from the start to Ramsey, he'd gain from there to the hilltops, and then we'd clock the same times back to the start. It was a nail-biter. In '66, in the 500, I came second to him by just two seconds after 360 km of racing... However, on the last lap in '67 I arrived at Ramsey with a good lead. He came back at me in the hills, but didn't gain too much, and I won more time off him on the descent, perhaps two seconds. I had an eight-second lead and there were only a few bends to go. I came out of a curve onto a long straight – and the chain snapped. I was sobbing in despair when I got back to the paddocks. He overtook me, and not just on the stopwatch, I mean he physically passed by – and won. I had to get off the bike and push it along a stretch of flat ground. Some fans rushed to help; but withdrawal was inevitable. Other fans found the broken chain. It had been a record-breaking race that had had everyone on the edge of their seats. When we arrived, the shoulders on our black leathers had turned white – we'd scraped along the chalk walls. When Hailwood took the podium he looked almost miserable, because he knew he'd won through my misfortune, not his own skill. I think he showed great sensitivity that day. I left, but the pain was eased by the company of a beautiful girl, who I already knew: she shouldn't really have come away with me, as she had her own problems. But seeing me so depressed she decided to go with me. Of course, it gave my morale a much needed boost. I'd been courting her for some time. Perhaps the disappointment of the race was what had been needed to draw us closer together. Anyway, that evening Hailwood dropped by to pick me up. He insisted that I go out and have a good time with him. He took me to a party in the Jaguar that belonged to his father, Stanley, who would have the girlfriend of the moment do the chauffeuring: they were all young, beautiful women – but the important thing was they could drive. Hailwood had an odd relationship with his father: when Mike didn't win he received harsh words of reproach. Anyway, we went along to a pub where there was music, food and dancing. Jim Redman was also there with his wife, a fantastic woman, and there were other riders. Wine, women and song it was. Hailwood had wanted me to go along because he saw me as the true winner of the race. We had a great time. Afterwards, Hailwood drove me and the girls back home. He scared the living daylights out of me on the way back, because he was absolutely smashed and his driving was appalling. I was terrified we'd end up in the sea. You know, even now I don't really like being a passenger in a car: but that time I was genuinely frightened. Miraculously, we arrived safe and sound.

The real sadness made itself felt later on, when I realised how things had gone. Such a close-run race could never be repeated: both of us with the bit between our teeth, our knuckles bloodied and the material skinned from the shoulder pads of out suits. He had a better engine with the Honda, I a better frame with the MV: it was a *beautiful* race. Prince Phillip had been watching. The race left an indelible memory because we were at the TT, because we were two of the best battle-hardened riders in the world, because it was a head-to-head for the motorcycle builders and because, as the gap swung from being in my favour to his and back again, we broke every record. The fans had gone wild: it was a dream, but in the end a broken one. It would have been the first big victory of my career. Moreover, two riders had died the day before. The atmosphere was spine-tingling. During the race I should have opened the tap on a small tank that drips oil onto the chain: however, you had to be careful not to open it too wide otherwise the oil would get on the tyres. Being a rider back then had its inconveniences. For example you had to wipe your goggles with a sponge, because after just one lap you couldn't see a thing. The sponge had to be kept in a special container to keep it moist: once, it popped out and dried up and I kept having to spit on it to keep the goggles clean – all while travelling at 280-300 kph, without the signposts there are now. For instance, just after the start, at Bray Hill, you'd arrive at the end of a straight and have to take a certain line. If you got it wrong, especially on the first lap when you were heavy with fuel and oil, the sump would hit the tarmac and risked being split. That's where Leslie Graham(1) died: the front forks hit a dip and he lost control of the bike.

Nao found Agostini's sadness moving. He imagined him at the end of that race he'd so deserved to win: frustrated, disappointed and embittered. In Nao's eyes, his defeat made him more human, more agreeable, less infallible.

Once again, he'd been surprised at how Agostini narrated success and defeat, celebration and disappointment in the same way. He wasn't a cold man, even though he might seem it. He always spoke with the same tone, quickly as if afraid of wasting time. But his talk of feelings and disappointment had conveyed much of what he'd felt at certain times, and this realisation drew Nao a little closer to his subject.

He restarted the tape.

NAO Who was the girl you were with after the race?
GIACOMO An English girl. She'd just got married. I'd already met her at a race in the UK. Just one smile and I was hooked. She was stunning, twenty-two years old, tall, blond, a pro tennis player and as sharp as a pin. She was already in a relationship and so we developed one of those knife-edge friendships made up of glances,

NOTE:(1) Leslie Graham (GB, 1911), the 500 cc World Champion in 1949 and winner of eight Grand Prix in 125, 350 and 500, died in the 1953 TT on an MV Agusta.

smiles and caresses. Yet we were besotted with each other, and I think my defeat that day broke down her defences. She saw how utterly shattered I was and just couldn't help but soften. After that race, for the very first time, we spent the night together.

NAO Odd. Love through defeat... Did you have a lot of women at the time?

GIACOMO Let's say, yes, quite a lot. It was a bit like being a sailor and having a girl in every port. Yet this girl was smarter than most and it was something... special.

NAO Tell me about Hailwood? Did you consider him a friend?

GIACOMO He was quite open, sociable, but would always make you feel a bit uneasy. Yes, he was a friend, but not the sort that hugs you or openly displays his affection. He was very English in that regard. Yet he was always a friend to me, even though, of course, his career came first. Early on in 1965 I was MV's golden boy, the young Italian the team had taken to heart, the one they had a special relationship with. This was probably because, as Italians, we had an instinctive feel for one other. I think Hailwood felt he had been put aside. It's often the way: when you join a foreign team you always feel a bit out of place. Yet he accepted it: if he was invited out, for instance, he accepted immediately, he wouldn't complain about having to get up early or anything. I think that the generally accepted image of him - a hell-raiser who was often drunk and couldn't give a damn - is an unfair one. For instance, in '67, just two days before the all-important TT, I called him up to see if he wanted to go for a drink. By nine he was back in his room, perfectly relaxed and in his pyjamas. One of his favourite pastimes was making models of motorcycles: he'd sometimes be doing that when everyone thought he was out on the tiles. If there was something serious to be done he was committed to the core. Other times, when he had more slack, he'd let himself go. I think his relationship with his father was essential to him: Stan pushed him hard. Whenever Hailwood wasn't leading a race Stan would - and I've witnessed this personally - be on the sidelines urging him to go faster because he was 'only' second. He'd drive him too hard. My, father, instead, would say "Slow down!". On the track he was tough, fast but never unfair. He never plotted against other riders and he didn't need to. If he won it was because he was the better rider, because he gave it everything he had. If he lost it was because someone else had ridden better. I've always admired opponents with that sense of fairness. He wanted to win for what he was. He didn't want races given to him. He detested the idea of winning through deviousness.

NAO Hailwood and you were two of the greatest Tourist Trophy racers ever.

GIACOMO He notched up fourteen victories in TT, I managed to win ten times. I used to tell people it was nine times until I read in a magazine and that I'd won ten times. When I checked my notes I realised they were right.

NAO Why did Hailwood decide to race cars after Honda left the scene? Had he spoken about it with you?

GIACOMO No. Like I said, he was pleasant and friendly, but riders will often develop mutual regard instead of close friendships. At the end of the day you're rivals, and that leaves little space for true companionship because that takes heart. To defeat someone takes a pinch of harshness, the killer instinct.

NAO So no sentiment then.

GIACOMO It's the exception, not the rule.

NAO Did you experience any exceptions of that kind?

GIACOMO No. Maybe no-one does.

NAO Why did Phil Read have such a bad reputation?

GIACOMO Because he was a hard case and, unlike Hailwood, he didn't care how he won. He wasn't overly keen on fair play. To him it was winning that counted: it didn't matter how. Read[1] would also try to destroy his rivals psychologically. With me, for instance, he'd do his utmost to put me on edge. His personality even gave his own team headaches: he'd argue with Bill Ivy all the time. But he never, ever gave up: he was always aggressive and always held on, waiting to pounce in case you screwed up or lost your concentration. Even if he was losing a second a lap he would never ease up: if anything, he'd go even harder, piling on the pressure to make you screw up. He didn't care about you at all. Read and Hailwood might have both been English, but they were very different people. It should be remembered that they'd started doing the TT on the 500 at the age of just eighteen, while we had to rise up through the 125, 175 and then the 250. By starting the TT on a 500 you learnt – and hardened – fast. For us, getting used to bigger, heavier bikes was a gradual process and this ini-

NOTE:[1] Phil Read (GB, 1939) won the 125 cc World Championship in '68, the 250 cc World Championship in 1964-65-68-71 and the 500 in 1973 and '74. He totalled 52 GP wins.

tially put us at a disadvantage. So at a certain point I bought myself a heavy bike, a Triumph, which I got in England, because the MV, especially the first 500 that Surtees, Gary Hocking and Hailwood raced with, weighed a ton. It was very difficult to control. With the Triumph I learnt to ride with my muscles rather than the finesse needed on the lighter bikes with their small pear-shaped tyres. Ubbiali and Provini taught me the importance of hunkering down behind the fairing and squashing yourself against the fuel tank. Just look at some of the photos from the time and you'll see what I mean. The bikes had little power, yet the circuits were more or less the same as they are today. Imagine doing the straight at Monza: today it takes less than ten seconds. Then it was half a minute. Thirty seconds, locked into each others' slipstreams. Today, you barely get into top gear before it's time to start braking again. Once, you'd get into fifth or sixth and sit there for anything up to a minute, so catching the slipstream of the bike in front was crucial. Now there's more power, the circuits are shorter, narrower, with one bend after another. On some tracks you don't even get to use fifth gear.

NAO Very few motor-racing champions become true champions, that is, champions who have come to personify an era, to dominate on the track and within their own teams. I've come to the conclusion that a real champion, one who wins and wins again, is the one who has absolute control of a team: a rider who is always Number One and always has a Number Two as his right-hand man, one who is always head and shoulders above anyone else in his team. There are plenty of examples of this in motor-racing, from Alberto Ascari, who formed a near-permanent partnership with Gigi Villoresi, to Jim Clark, who crushed the opposition, practically making it run and hide. Look at Michael Schumacher, who's never wanted anything more than a dependable Number Twos such as Eddie Irvine and Rubens Barrichello on the team. Then there was Niki Lauda:, when he had team-mates at his own level, such as Clay Regazzoni and Alain Prost, he ended up in difficulty. Same with motorcycling: throughout almost all your career you were the team's Number One and nobody with your level of talent was ever able to get their hands on the same bike you used. What I'm trying to say is that this appears to be a constant with all the great champions. Look at Valentino Rossi: he's never wanted a strong team-mate.

GIACOMO Let me explain. First of all, great talents are a rarity, to the extent that if you remove the big talent everybody else suddenly looks good: Valentino Rossi, who's just arrived at Yamaha and takes a second off his closest rivals with every lap[1], is the obvious example. Then, finding two great talents with similar characteristics is no easy task either, because a great talent comes along once every ten years, if that. Finally, even if two great talents appear at the same time, what possible reason could they have to join the same team and start arguing and competing among themselves when they can both go to different teams and each be the Number One in those teams?. The manufacturers have nothing to gain either: two talents cost twice as much as one, while a second, less skilled rider offers a more economical package and will probably yield a similar number of wins anyway. It's only logical that there be one talent per team. Journalists will often kick up a fuss because they think that the 'great champion' can't bare to have an opponent of the same calibre, that he wants to keep on winning and maintain control: well, of course he does! It's only natural that a great champion will have no desire to move to a team already occupied by someone just as sharp. He'll go elsewhere. Also, the manufacturer is unlikely to want to pay the newcomer anywhere near as much money as the champion they've already got. And since only one of them can win it makes more sense to have a 'second' to help the champion keep on winning while costing the team less money.

NAO Which puts the champion at his ease, I imagine?

GIACOMO Well…. Look at how it went between me and Hailwood, in '65: when he realised I'd become the focus of things, he soon started looking for another team where he'd be the centre of attention, and he found it with Honda.

NAO But if you think about it, very few riders have dominated both an epoch and a team, have been the absolute Number One. There was you, and now there's Valentino Rossi…

GIACOMO Like I said, great riders aren't born every week. Checa looked good, Melandri looked good – but Valentino Rossi puts a second into them every lap. They're good riders, he's a *great* racer. It's always been like that: the champion has few rivals, otherwise he wouldn't be a champion. While the races might sometimes be more interesting without these dominating talents it also has to be said

NOTE:[1] Valentino Rossi (Urbino, 1979) is the only rider in the world to have won a world title in four different categories: 125, 250, 500 and MotoGP. In 2004 he won with Yamaha after being with Honda since 2000. So far (2004) he has won six world championship titles and 68 grand prix races

that they give the race a distinctive allure.

NAO I'd like to talk about when you raced cars, something you rarely mention.

GIACOMO I got the opportunity to switch to cars early on. I was down at the Modena *aerautodromo*, testing the bikes, and Enzo Ferrari was there. He asked me if I wanted to try one of his cars, if I'd ever thought of racing them. I was flattered by his question, put to me by the great man in person, so I tried out a Ferrari Dino. The test seemed to go quite well. Later on we ran into each other again and Ferrari told me that if I ever wanted to race cars he'd have one waiting for me. Yet there were other things to consider: I was at the peak of my motorcycling career, I'd already won the World Championship several times, my team was letting me take some of the technical decisions, I was the prince of things and I was looked after and listened to by everyone. I would have had to leave everything that had taken so long to build and start out in Formula 1 from scratch. So I turned it down. Only at the end of my career, when I already knew that my riding heyday was over, after being in tears for three days, did I start looking for something to plug the appalling gap I knew the end of my two-wheeled career would leave. Just like anyone else who retires, the lack of meaningful employment drives you nuts because you just feel like you're marking time, waiting to die. I felt so miserable about the whole thing that I decided, since racing car drivers generally prolong their careers more than motorcycle riders do, I might as well give it a go. My sponsor, Marlboro, reckoned the switch to be an attention-grabber, so they backed my decision and I made my debut in Formula 2. It was 1978, the year in which my fellow countryman, Giacomelli, dominated. It wasn't easy to forget everything I'd learnt about motorcycles and start from scratch. It took time. I was with the Trivellato team, which had looked good to me. The car was a Chevron. Only later did I realise that I'd chosen or, rather, bought a car that was - as Patrese had said when I sought his opinion - difficult to drive, like a go-kart: you had to slam it up against the kerb, drive it obliquely into the corners. I was already a pro and had been used to a more technical approach - skimming the kerb, never touching it, exiting the bends at high revs. I never really got to grips with that car. When I got the chance to try the March I realised it was far better. It was with a March that Giacomelli has won the European Formula 2 title that same year. He'd said it was the car for me, even if I did drive like I was still on a motorcycle. For example, I'd go into the curve slow and come out of it with the engine screaming. My engines were the highest-revving of the lot. Word got around that Marlboro had made sure I was given special engines, but that simply wasn't true: I came out of the bends faster but went into them far too slowly. In a car you have to enter the bend at high speed, obliquely, with plenty of power. I was used to the low horsepower of a motorcycle: in the bend I'd rev up the engine ready to make the most of it on the straight. In Formula 1 it's even worse: you have to go right into the bend and then block the car, with the wheels almost at standstill, then slam the accelerator to the floor and roar off again, because with 700 HP you've got all the power you need to get going. Instead, I'd go into the bend smoothly, keeping the engine revs high, so I'd come out of the bend at 8500 rpm as opposed to, say, 8000 rpm. On a motorcycle this makes sense: not in a car, though. With the March, which was a somewhat smoother vehicle, more of a pro's car, you could skim the kerb. It was more refined, more technical. But by then I was getting pretty disappointed by the results and I'd had enough. Then I got the opportunity to try my hand at Formula 1: they'd organised a championship in England called Aurora, which used Formula 1 cars from the previous season. I bought myself two Williams and entered the fray. Without any great deal of practice, mind you, as I received the cars only at the last minute. I had fun and learnt a lot but I didn't have much success. Things improved the following year, as the results testify. They would have been even better if I'd bought cars with skirts, which were at least a second a lap faster. But since I'd bought two Formula 1 cars the year before, which I couldn't sell on as they'd been rendered virtually obsolete by the skirted models, I was forced to race at a disadvantage. Even so, I still kept coming in third, fourth or fifth. That was 1980. I was doing all right. If I'd had a bit more success I would no doubt have been happier, but I have to admit that by then my real career was over and I no longer had any great ambitions.

NAO But you did get your first experience as team manager. You brought in the sponsors, found the cars…

GIACOMO Yes, but it was just a small team, based in Britain: there was a workshop with five or six mechanics, of which three were for me. They had the lorry and drove the cars to the track for me.

NAO Did you let other drivers race as well?

GIACOMO Since I had two cars, yes. I used to rent one out to absorb the expenses a bit. However, I wouldn't say that was my first team management experience.

NAO What happened next?

GIACOMO In 1980 I enjoyed racing the cars a lot more. I didn't have much success, on account of the fact that my rivals' cars had skirts. With the right car, I reckon I could have started winning. We also had to economise: I didn't get much practice, couldn't rent a circuit to test, so my real training turned out to be in pre-race practice and qualifying. Getting results was no easy task. I knew I wasn't going to be World Champion, because I was at the end of my career, but I was keen to find out how a Formula 1 car was driven and I really enjoyed myself.

NAO So was 1980 the definitive end of your racing career?

GIACOMO Yes. I didn't do anything in 1981, I just looked about, weighing up opportunities for the future. Then a friend of mine, Giancarlo Spezia, manager of Marlboro Italia, suggested I manage a motorcycling team. I was still tied to Marlboro, so I went along to Yamaha to ask for the bikes: I suggested that they take care of technical development and that I handle all the expenses, organisation, transfers, the riders and the on-track bike management. They accepted, so I succeeded in creating my own Motorcycling World Championship team.

NAO How did it go?

GIACOMO I'll be honest. I wasn't too enthusiastic about it at the start. Then I got more and more into it and realised the whole thing was giving me immense satisfaction. I would never have thought I'd get tearful on seeing one of my motorcycles come first, but I did. It wasn't quite the same as winning yourself, but managing a team to victory was a very special sort of fulfilment. I won three world titles in the 500, in '84, '86 and '88.

NAO Would you agree that your best riders were Roberts(1), Lawson(2) and Spencer(3)?

GIACOMO Yes, but Spencer was a disaster because I thought he'd have the same grit he had when he stopped racing for Honda;

NOTE:(1) Kenny Roberts (USA, 1951) won three World Championships in the 500 class (1978-79-80) and 24 GPs. (2) Eddie Lawson (USA 1958) won four World Championships in the 500 (1984-86-88-89) and 31 GPs. (3) Freddie Spencer (USA 1961) won two World Championship titles in the 500 (1983-85) and one in the 250 (1985), totalling 27 GP wins.

unfortunately psychological problems were afoot. He'd also had a bad fall and his arm had swollen up because of circulation problems. Yet the core of the problem lay elsewhere. When he didn't even show up at the first test session I immediately realised he wasn't the go-getting rider he'd been with Honda. He'd had something of a meltdown previously, but no-one had given it much importance as he'd managed to cover it up. When, together with Marlboro, we invited him to a meeting in Losanna, he convinced us he'd had a physical problem and that it would pass. We took his word for it, but it wasn't so. At the first race he didn't even show up. He was wasting our time, and it was soon obvious that he wanted to worm money out of us without making an effort to get results. So I let him go before the season was even over. It was a huge disappointment.

NAO Yet Spencer had been a great champion.

GIACOMO Yes, that's true, but at a certain point he collapsed psychologically and he was never quite the same again. For example, I noticed he'd say lots of things, which, in the end, turned out to be a pack of lies.

NAO Lawson, instead, was quite different, wasn't he?

GIACOMO Yes, he was very serious. Spencer was better than Lawson but Lawson was much smarter. He'd prepare himself meticulously and he thoroughly deserved his four world titles. He knew how to set up the motorcycle, put his heart into preparation, gave one hundred percent all the time. It was his approach to life in general. He was serious before the race – and serious after it, and could be crabby and cantankerous too: he was presumptuous, doubtful and envious, especially of me. "Here comes Mr. fifteen-times world-champion", he'd often jibe. My fifteen world titles riled him. I'd fire back with "Yes, he does, Eddie, you are not mistaken".

NAO What was Kenny Roberts like?

GIACOMO As fast as lightning but perhaps a bit weak psychologically, because Spencer's arrival annoyed him. Roberts was highly ambitious. I mean, consider this: when I went to Daytona for the first time in '74, General Motors sent a driver in a white, two-seater Corvette Stingray to pick me up at the airport. The side of the car sported the legend "Giacomo Agostini, 13 Times World Champion", the number of championships I'd clocked up by then. Kenny Roberts was inflamed by this, declaring that he, not Agostini, was the World Champion. Because, said Roberts, America was the world, not Europe, and since he was American, he was the

World Champion. Yes, a bit ambitious, I reckon.

NAO How did Roberts manage, in the late seventies, manage to beat much younger, highly motivated adversaries such as Johnny Cecotto[(1)], Barry Sheene[(2)] and Randy Mamola[(3)]?

GIACOMO Kenny Roberts had a second-per-lap margin over the others. He was, quite simply, above them. He was one of the best I've ever seen, had the same sort of class displayed by Valentino Rossi now. He might not have obtained the same results, for a number of reasons, or on account of having made different choices, but on the bike he was almost unbeatable.

NAO Which Italians did you have on your team?

GIACOMO Luca Cadalora, who was leading the World Championship in the 250 cc class, and Paolo Casoli, with one year's experience on a semi-private motorcycle. So we couldn't expect much. Virginio Ferrari, who I prefer not to talk about. Then there was Graziano Rossi: I gave him the official Yamaha at a race in Imola where he fell and gave us all the fright of our lives. Cadalora was outstanding, a powerhouse: he had a great year with us and the only reason he didn't win the championship was that we ran into an ultra-sharp Kocinski. Ah, I nearly forgot Doriano Romboni: I'd set up a 250 team for him, with a semi-official Honda. Romboni was fast: in Brazil he won hands down but at other times he would get demoralised and fail to bring home the points. It was, instead, necessary to face the problems, solve them and move on.

NAO After the glut of Italians in 1979-82, with Ferrari[(4)], Rossi, Lucchinelli[(5)] and Uncini[(6)], why did the Italians suddenly disappear from the 500 cc class?

GIACOMO Because, as I've already said, great champions aren't born every day. We had to wait twenty years for Valentino Rossi to come along.

NAO After Yamaha you moved to Cagiva.

GIACOMO With Eddie Lawson and Kocinski, yes. And as team

NOTE:[(1)] Johnny Cecotto (Venez. 1956) was the first World Champion from the American continent: in '75 he won the 350 title; he won a total of 14 GPs.[(2)] Barry Sheene (GB 1950) won the 500 cc World Championship in 1976 and '77 and 23 GPs.[(3)] Randy Mamola (USA, 1959) came second in the 500 cc World Championship four times between 1980 and 1987, winning 13 GPs.[(4)] Virginio Ferrari (1952) came second in the 500 cc class in '79.[(5)] Marco Lucchinelli (1954) won the 500 cc World Championship in '81.[(6)] Franco Uncini (1955) the same title in 1982.

manager I had the satisfaction of giving Cagiva their first World Championship win, a victory in which my own experience proved essential. We were at Budapest, with Eddie Lawson. There had just been the most incredible downpour, barely a minute before the start, and the sky still looked threatening. I told him to mount the slicks. He was the only one to do so: all the others had their wet weather tyres. Since I knew winning on an even footing was going to be a tough proposition I thought our only chance was to go against the grain. If the weather cleared we'd win hands down. On the first, second and third laps Lawson was trailing in last place. After seven or eight laps the sun came through, the tarmac started to dry, and he rose up through the field to take the lead. We had another excellent two years after that, and if Cagiva hadn't withdrawn we could have done a lot more. I would have focussed on John Kocinski, an incredibly competitive youngster, a motorcycling animal.

NAO Is the racing world a difficult one, from the team manager's viewpoint?

GIACOMO Up to a point. I think I found relations with the riders the most difficult part. I knew the job inside out, knew what had to be done on the track, the preparation it required, what went through their minds. They couldn't lie to me: riders can be a bit sneaky at times, perhaps cover things up; we whinge because we want to shine all the time and the motorbike doesn't always let you. When the fast lap times aren't coming we blame the bike. Yet because I'd done the job for years, I knew immediately when a rider was trying to pull the wool over my eyes; that rider would then feel uneasy with me 'cause he knew I knew all the tricks and there was no point in him trying it on. Many a time, though, I tried to make them understand that my advice wasn't just for my own good but also theirs: our concerns were mutual, because we both wanted to win and both had to give it our all because our goals were the same.

NAO Is it a political environment?

GIACOMO It didn't use to be. More so, these days, perhaps, because of the sponsors. Yet I'd still say our sport is a healthy one, run by fine people.

Nao switched off the player: the tape had ended. He felt a bit tired. He didn't ask himself (and he should have done) whether a life that revolved around work was a healthy one. He just couldn't conceive of or see an alternative. Work had allowed him to go and live on his own, to leave the provinces for the city, buy a home, find a niche for himself. Work had given him everything, nothing else came close. That was why he couldn't see anything that might represent an alternative, a way out of the endless commitments. Work was a fact of life, almost comforting in its certainty. And he was at an age in which you need to focus on work, to build for the future. Nao had a traditionally linear view of life: first a man establishes a career, creates a cushion of wealth, then a family with the right woman. There was no need to hurry. Aware of this, he was not at all stressed. He was, well, just a bit *tired*, because he'd been working so hard: but all said and done it was what he wanted. He enjoyed it.

Nevertheless, that weekend he'd visit his parents and take it easy. Because his dedication to work during the week was only matched by his non-dedication to it on Saturdays and Sundays.

He came from a provincial town with a provincial lifestyle, its slow but steady pace marked by routine, a few ceremonies here and there and rather a lot of horseplay. That was where Nao had been modelled, in an unchanging world with no future and no past because nothing ever happened – or, rather, a thousand things of no particular importance happened. All the important stuff had happened centuries ago. It was now a town mostly populated by the elderly, the young having moved to the bigger towns and cities in search of work, returning only at weekends to see their families. Nao himself went back every weekend, mainly because he didn't know where else to go and also because he felt comfortable there, managed to relax and it didn't cost him a penny. At most he'd eat out with some friends in some cheap but cheerful *trattoria*.

He'd go and see his Mum, an apprehensive woman who always made a fuss of him. Each time he'd complain about her being so soft, but secretly he adored the attention and the feel-good factor it generated. Sometimes he'd yell at her (he never yelled at anyone, but he did with his mother, just as he did when he was a boy), and then he'd laugh for having been so absurd.

Her cuisine was the rich, heavy food of local tradition but, being a big eater, he didn't hold back. It sometimes took him a couple of days to digest her heavy offerings but to Nao it was just another aspect of the love-hate relationship he had with his family, his mother and his home town.

He spent a lot of time in the bar. Sunday he'd take a stroll around the *piazza*, then watch the Sunday afternoon football matches on TV.

There was also plenty of dozing. He sometimes went out with boyhood friends and half the time they'd end up talking about their childhood, the tricks they played on each other, the acts of bravado that worried their parents and sometimes even the townsfolk. They were typical male friendships that continued out of inertia; each man shielded the other from the awareness that they really had nothing better to do. Friendships born out of the dullness of the provinces, creating a mutual support network among people who have no idea what they're doing or where they're going, yet continue to stay exactly where they are, terrified of making a mistake and fouling things up. It was a sorry situation ,would they but realise it.

On Sunday evening he drove back to Milan. He preferred to leave late (sometimes after dinner, sometimes *without* dinner if the lunch had been particularly heavy) to avoid the traffic. He knew the route back by heart. Each time he'd note down how long the trip took him so he could compare it to the previous times.

Tape n° 4
The joy of winning

Nao's days passed by, each the same as the last. The drive to work, the day at the editorial office, the coffee machine, the banter, flattering the boss, a laugh with the latest receptionist, the midday sandwich with colleagues, the computer (which was fast becoming his window on the world), the afternoon hours that sometimes flashed by and sometimes crawled, the drive home.

Whenever there was a car to be test-driven and the director decided to send an editor as opposed to an external, it was a breath of fresh air, almost a free holiday. On those occasions Nao would stuff himself in the best restaurants and stay at the most luxurious hotels. He'd smoke fat Cuban cigars and take on the important air of a man self-satisfied with his lot. Before retiring to his room, he'd sip a little whisky, an exclusive single malt from the Orkneys.

Over the last two days he'd been in Germany for the presentation of a new economy car. He'd joked with his colleagues, done a bit of networking, eaten and drunk well and made himself almost too comfortable. On Wednesday morning, his face carrying its usual smile, he returned to his usual routine: the alarm clock, the editorial office and all the rest. And waiting in the wings of his workaday world, was of, course, Giacomo Agostini.

GIACOMO Let me tell you about when I was a guest of Fernand Marcos, the President of the Philippines, and his wife Imelda. What a week that was. A supper was held in Mindanao, Imelda's birthplace: they had this stunning beachside villa there. We flew in by helicopter and when we arrived a huge crowd was waiting because she'd always arrive with hundred of gifts. As Imelda exited the helicopter, in fact, she started distributing T-shirts and trousers to the poor people of the island. Another evening she organised a supper on a yacht. After a certain hour the curfew came into force: a siren would sound and the city went dead. Only government cars were allowed out, to allow us to make the transfer from the presidential palace. Each car had a red light on the hood so the police could instantly recognise it as part of the president's motorcade. Anyway, that evening on the yacht, towards one or two in the morning, the President and Imelda took their leave: almost as soon as they left dozens of armed police officers came out of the hold to escort them. I hadn't even realised they were there.

NAO How come they invited you?

GIACOMO Some friends of mine from Rome had organised the trip. Gina Lollobrigida and other celebrities were there, including the children of Niarchos, the famous Greek ship-builder. It was Christmas, and on Christmas Day everyone was given a wad of money. I was quite amazed. I mean, a wad of money is always welcome – but when I saw it was also being given to Niarchos' children, who'd arrived in their own Boeing 727, it did seem just a tad over the top. Anyway, they took the cash like everyone else and went off to spend it in the shops. We all did.

NAO What were Marcos and his wife Imelda like?

GIACOMO He was as hard as nails and she wasn't exactly a shrinking violet either. You could see it was her who ruled the roost.

NAO If you try to imagine their faces, what comes to mind?

GIACOMO Imelda was beautiful, impressive, of strong character. She made me feel uneasy. He had a the face of a bully – but whether he really was or not I have no idea. I suppose it was the kind of face you have to have if you're a dictator.

NAO Did success bring a lot of invitations like these?

GIACOMO You bet it did. I was the man of the moment. I expect that Marcos and his wife enjoyed having me as their guest. I was on a roll: I'd already notched up a few World Championship titles, my photo was in all the magazines. I got a call from Mario D'Urso, a close friend of the Marcos family, he invited me along and I accepted immediately. "Why not?", I said. Our party of eight or ten people also included Prince Giovannelli. We had a marvellous week. And I'm still proud of having accepted that invitation, because that supper at the Palace, as the invitee of a President, is something that I am unlikely ever to forget.

NAO Did you have a lot of experiences of this sort?

GIACOMO Yes. I remember the première of a film starring Alain

World Champions inevitably seem to be surrounded by women.
Lucia, Agostini's partner for many years, stands in the background as he talks to Marika, the wife of a close friend.

Mike Hailwood and Giacomo Agostini at Riccione get to know two glamorous-looking sisters from Emilia-Romagna and invite them along to the post-race partying.

Wherever the champion went, women were never far away. Above, with two friends. Below, from left: Agostini, Lucia, Marika and Prince Giovanelli.

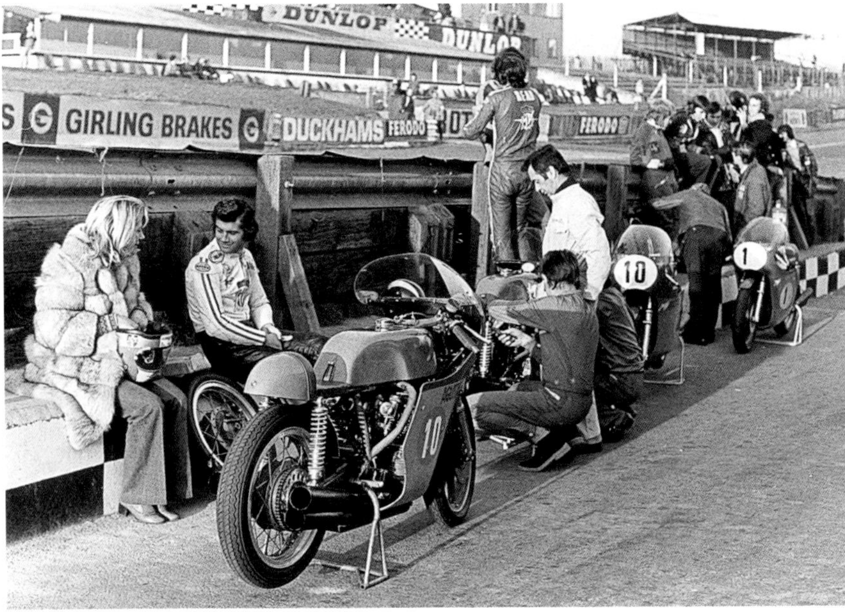

Enzo Ferrari frowned on the presence of women in the paddocks, but motorcycling has always welcomed them. Above: qualifying at Brands Hatch. Below: at Monza.

Daytona, 1974: after a clamorous victory in the 200 Mile Race with Yamaha, an exhausted Agostini shares his joy with Lucia.

Agostini takes to the snow with a French girlfriend during the inter-season winter break.

Life as a legend: countless gala evenings in dark suit and tie, and never alone.
Endless beauty queens were met on the podium - and off it.

Another girlfriend from Agostini's racing years. The role of the champion's girl was – and always has been – one of the hardest to play.

Agostini hits the silver screen: the scene above is from the 1971 flick *Bolidi sull'asfalto a tutta birra*. He also starred in *Amore Formula 2* and *Formula 1 Nell'inferno del Grand Prix*.

Above: a scene from one of the films Agostini starred in between 1970 and 1971.
Below: with two other motorcycling giants, Phil Read (middle) and Jarno Saarinen (right).

Above: Ago heads for the start with his friend Bonetti, known as "The Boss", and MV's racing manager, Magni (right). Below: surrounded by photographers (faithful friend Lucio Castelli is second from left).

MV is the past, Yamaha the future: here Ago challenges up-and-coming talent Barry Sheene (Suzuki) at the Assen circuit in Holland.

Two stroke or four-stroke, it made no difference. Giacomo Agostini just kept on winning and with Yamaha would once again be World Champion.

War and Peace. Above: Agostini pushes his Yamaha 750 to the limit.
Below: enjoying the meat carved by Imelda Marcos in the Philippines.

Above: with father Aurelio, mother Maria Vittoria and Lucia. Below: on the Yamaha 750, the motorcycle that would give Ago his last victory in 1977.

A dyed-in-the-wool Agostini fan from Holland proudly displays a chest tattoo of Agostini riding his Yamaha.

Delon, who was a friend of mine. He'd wanted some 'seconds' along with him for a Paris première and he'd chosen myself and Monzon, the boxer who had himself just won a world title. First I went to Alain's house in the centre of Paris, then we headed for the Théâtre des Champs-Élysées in a Rolls-Royce, escorted by police. We turned up half an hour later than anticipated, but I think that was just part of the show. There must have been a hundred photographers in the foyer and flashguns were going off everywhere; Alain Delon was France's most famous actor, I'd been World Champion more than ten times and Monzon was certainly no nobody either. You can imagine the interest and enthusiasm. Just to brighten things up we were accompanied by four or five stunning girls, actresses who'd been called in by Alain Delon. Whenever he was looking for co-stars or extras there'd be a long line of girls outside his office, each more beautiful than the last. His secretary would ditch those she thought weren't up to the mark and then let the others through. So he had a whole clutch of beautiful women at his beck and call - another reason why he was such a good friend. The première was attended by all the 'right' people of Paris, of course, and his long-standing companion, Mireille Darc, was there too. After a long welcoming applause, we settled down to watch the film and afterwards dined out at a club. There was a gorgeous girl with us. "She's the one for you", Alain said to me. She really was striking, a stunning blonde. We had an enjoyable evening, but I was grossly mistaken about its outcome: in the end she left with another woman.

NAO When did you meet Alain Delon?

GIACOMO It was in Rome when I was doing TV ads for API. He was there for work too. I only met him fleetingly, we didn't become friends straight away. Nevertheless, because he was a sports fan, especially boxing and motorcycling, he wanted Monzon and I to accompany him to that première. It was an unforgettable evening: it had a fairytale quality to it, even if, in the end, the disappointment of going home alone stung a bit.

NAO All the time you were racing, you thought of women as one of life's pleasant rewards, as another form of entertainment. Isn't that so?

GIACOMO To me, women have always been one of the things that make life worth living. I've always been attracted to their company.

NAO Sure, but I get the feeling that during this period they were one of life's accessories. A bit like a fine meal, as it were.

GIACOMO No, it was definitely much more than that. Yet to me it was a pleasure that had to be separated from my career. Other riders gave their women tasks and responsibilities, yet I don't think this is ever a good idea for the sportsman. An athlete needs to be focussed: he doesn't want suggestions or distractions. In my opinion it's extremely difficult for a woman to help you in an active sense. I mean, she helps you just by being there, keeping you relaxed: but she shouldn't be demanding. If I was with women who didn't understand this, I'd get tetchy. They just couldn't grasp what a rider went through before the start, didn't realise that he can't allow himself even the slightest distraction, and certainly not a lovers' tiff. An athlete should never be contradicted before the moment of a competition, even if he's talking bollocks. Like I said, a woman can help an athlete towards greatness, but she can also push him towards destruction. I've only ever had girlfriends. I never committed myself to a woman because my job came first. I never listened to the advice of any woman: I didn't want it and wouldn't accept it. She wasn't there to play a leading role.

NAO Did you ever cry when you were racing, because of a victory or a defeat?

GIACOMO I cried when I won my first world title at Monza. I cried the Monday after Monza on account of the deaths of Pasolini and Saarinen. I cried when my chain snapped at the TT and I rolled down the hills in neutral, my crash helmet resting on the tank. I cried when I lost my world title in Japan, because I virtually had it in my hand when I was stopped by a faulty condenser. I cried when Lawson won his first title and I was Yamaha team manager. I cried when Lawson won the first race on a Cagiva. I cried for three days when I hung up my helmet. I've also cried because of woman: but I'm not saying who.

Nao stopped the tape. Yes, Ago had surprised him here. Nao would have bet that no woman had ever made him cry. But he'd been wrong: Ago had said so himself and there was no reason to doubt him.

Women. They had been a constant throughout Ago's life. Nao remembered Agostini telling him about how Randy Mamola, on discovering that his girlfriend had left him, had burst into tears and had wanted to stop racing and return home to America. It was hard to imagine any such reaction from Agostini: he might have cried for a woman, but he'd never been controlled by one. He'd said so. It occurred to him that Mamola had never won a world title despite coming second four times. Giacomo Agostini had won *fifteen* world championships.

Nao remembered the advice he'd given a friend who had been shattered by the end of a relationship. "What's wrong?", he'd offered. "Is it a health, money or work problem? If not, then you can rest easy: it's nothing that can't be put right".

NAO You met a great many celebrities. Tell me about Gianni Agnelli.

GIACOMO I met him once in Monza, when I was testing. He was just passing by, perhaps because they'd been testing the Ferrari that morning, and he dropped by to say hello. I met him other times, in Rome, always by chance, never on formal occasions. Once I ran into him on the island of Cavallo in Corsica, and I jokingly told him off because one of the friends at his table was a former girlfriend of mine from Paris: "Dearest Giacomo", he said, "so *you* know them all as well, it seems". I pretended to be disgruntled because she'd abandoned me for the super-wealthy.

NAO Let's return to racing. How would you define the act of overtaking? How do you prepare for it?

GIACOMO If you're coming to the close of a race, then you take the time to study your opponent, seek out the best place to pass him, weed out his weaknesses. If, instead, the race is in its early stages, you overtake more spontaneously, as and when opportunity arises. I think the former might be defined as 'real' overtaking, but studying your adversary cuts both ways because it can expose your own weaknesses and qualities. If he's behind, you'll show him how you take a certain bend and end up teaching him how to do it even better. This is crucial, something that has to be taken into account in the span of both a race and a career. You might try and trick him by overtaking at non-strategic points only, thus hiding your true intentions and teaching him nothing. Or you can stick the knife in on the last lap. Or you can take advantage of a mistake of his, overtaking and gaining ground quickly. When a rival's mistake comes unexpectedly, you sometimes end up overtaking without even intending to. So you take advantage of it: but if he then gets back on your tail and won't let you go, at that point you either throttle back or pretend to make small mistakes and lull him into a false sense of security. I remember when I was overtaken by Barry Sheene in Holland. Sheene and I were battling it out for final victory, he with his Suzuki, I with my Yamaha. On the last lap, three bends from the chequered flag, I glanced backwards and noticed he wasn't so close any more. Without even realising it I thought I had it in the bag. Psychologically, I softened, the edge was taken off my drive and aggression. Going into the last curve, it still looked like I couldn't lose, but I went into it slower than I would have done if I'd been fully focussed. Sheene slammed the ten-metre gap shut instantly and pipped me on the finishing line. It was a huge blow, and it'd all been my fault: I'd felt sure of myself and gone off the boil: without quite realising it I'd eased up for a moment and ruined it for myself. It was a learning experience, though: it never happened again.

NAO What's the best overtaking manoeuvre you can remember?

GIACOMO When I overtook Pasolini in Modena: he'd been on the verge of winning and the crowd went wild. I went for broke on the penultimate bend. At Modena it was like being in a stadium: you could see the entire circuit from any place in the stands. Like I said, he practically had it in his pocket, so I braked desperately late and hugged the inside edge of the bend. He went a little wide, instead: I was tucked in so far there was nowhere else to go. His fans protested, but it was demonstrated that I'd obstructed no-one: I'd braked late and hard, caught him and edged in front by a wheel; but because I was on the inside I came out of the bend first, denying him space. I certainly didn't push him and did nothing unfair. Then there was the time I overtook Phil Read: he was riding an MV, me a Yamaha. I caught him at the end of the straight at Hockenheim, on a sweeping bend at 170-180 kph: I passed him on the inside. Another memorable occasion was at the Solitude, my second world championship race with the Morini 250. I started off in the second row because I'd come fifth in qualifying, pitting a single-cylinder Morini against Hondas and Yamahas. All the big names were there: Jim Redman, Luigi Taveri, Phil Read. On the first, slightly raised bend, I overtook the leading quartet, all four world champions! It wasn't that I was the better rider: the motorcycle gave me an edge there because it was light; I had no idea about tyre temperatures at the time – I just threw myself into the bend with the footrests scraping the tarmac. On the straight, though, all four of them caught up and overtook me, because I only had 36 HP and they had fifty. Yet my machine was the more manageable. I remember that, between Hailwood and I, neither had the definitive upper hand over the other. In the beginning he had the edge because of his four or five years of experience. But I learned a lot in my first year, and after that overtaking each other was never easy: either he was having a good day and won, or I was having a good day and won.

NAO Did you gain a reputation as a late braker, a 'hard man'?

GIACOMO No, such epithets are rarely attributed to the greats. If a rider gets a tag like that it means he has this characteristic but not the others. A truly great rider, instead, is near-perfect all-round: he might not have breathtakingly late braking, but he does have a champion's braking; he doesn't drive the crowd wild when he takes a bend, he takes it like a champion. Those with outstanding characteristics night score a twelve on one count and a seven on another. The champion scores a consistent ten all round. Pasolini would, at races held in Emilia Romagna, brake spectacularly: but it never really yielded him much. I'd take things more smoothly: he'd put on more of a show but the end result was the same. It's a bit like side-skidding today: the bikes allow you to do it, but there are good riders and not-so-good riders. Being a good side-skidder doesn't necessarily make you faster. Sometimes, less side-skidding can give you the edge. It all depends on riding style. Valentino Rossi's side-skids are spectacular, but he gets results from them too because he rides a certain way, while another talent might not achieve the same results. Take McCoy, for instance: his side-skids used to amaze everyone but he won very few races. Biaggi might not be a great side-skidder but he has a clean style and zips along regardless.

NAO I'm rather struck by what you said about overtaking and not revealing your secrets. Since a rider might be racing against the same opponents for years, he has to ensure he teaches them as little as possible, keep his distance: if he's the champion, he has to fly high and let the others wallow in their inferiority.

GIACOMO Certainly, but you can't hide everything. Racing with champions, you can't help but learn. In the beginning I used to study Hailwood: when I switched from lightweight to heavy bikes I found myself in trouble, I needed experience. So I'd observe Hailwood and try to copy him. He wasn't like Provini or Ubbiali, who were always tucked behind the fairing. Like a lot of others (especially non-Italians) who were already used to riding heavy bikes he'd ride with a knee sticking out, his body breaking the outline of the bike. I'll always remember the pharmacist at Lovere, Dr. Rolla, almost a second father to me: I'd often meet up with him in his pharmacy after the races. He'd say, "See Hailwood? He shifts about, slips his body this way and that". Or, "That other guy…" - he'd only ever talk about the best - "does it like this". So I tried to forget what I'd learnt on the smaller bikes and adapt to the bigger ones, which were ridden with less grace.

NAO Which rider taught you the most?

GIACOMO Hailwood, although he never explained a thing – you don't teach your rivals. I observed him during the races and picked things up. Like I said: there's no real friendship between riders. There's respect – and maybe not even that any more – but you're always antagonists. If I can, I'll snatch victory from you: it can't be any other way.

NAO Did you prefer the 3-cylinder MV or the 4-cylinder?

GIACOMO In the 350 I preferred the four-cylinder, in the 500 the three-cylinder. Because in the 350 we'd managed to build a great four-cylinder, which hummed at 16,000 rpm: it was as finely tuned as a violin and the frame was perfect for it. Not so on the four-cylinder 500. The three-cylinder, instead, didn't have outstanding horsepower but did have the right frame; it was balanced, had good forks and superb braking and that blend meant you could squeeze one hundred percent out of it. We won because the bike was perfect.

NAO How was the MV 500 three-cylinder ridden?

GIACOMO All motorcycles are ridden the same way. A stiffer brake, a classier frame, but nothing changes really. The Yamaha was as good a ride as the MV was. Perhaps it was the Yamaha 350 that puzzled me the most: it had a small, twin-cylinder, lightweight engine. It didn't have a great deal of power but it clocked up great times, because even though it was a two-stroke and there was no engine brake, the disk brakes would still bring you to a quick halt. The engine was half the weight of its MV counterpart and the motorcycle was so light it felt you were on a bicycle. Imagine it: doing 250 kph with barely 30 kilos under the saddle. All the others had sixty kilos.

NAO How do you get the most from a motorcycle?

GIACOMO You take it to the edge, all the time, everywhere: you sit up as late as possible going into the bend, you brake as late as possible, throttle back as late as possible. Only with Surtees, Hailwood and Hocking's 4-cylinder 500 MVs did you ride differently. For example, the sweeping bend at Monza, where you'd arrive in sixth, couldn't be done at full throttle: you had to ease off the gas because fifth was too tight and sixth too slack: so you eased back a little and instead of taking it at 270 you'd do it at 255. When you eased off, though, the bike would start to twist and slow you down. I was still rather small, almost minute, and I just couldn't ride this brute the way I wanted to. It was John Surtees who provided the answer. "Instead of slowing down by throttling back", he said, "put your foot on the brake and slow down without decelerating, that way the bike'll stay in traction and won't warp". I did as he suggested and gained half a second a lap. It was an unusual bike, that one, and had to be dominated by sheer force.

NAO What went through your mind on a fast, sweeping bend?

GIACOMO I was so focussed I just used to stare at the tarmac and the rev counter. I thought whether I needed to change gear, whether the revs had dropped too much, if the track was dirty, if there was a stone or a patch of oil: I was so focussed I held my breath.

NAO Did you ever close your eyes, even for a fraction of a second?

GIACOMO No, no. On the contrary, tears would sometimes run down my cheeks as I strived to keep them open: I didn't want to miss a thing.

NAO Loris Capirossi has said that riding a motorbike on a sweeping bend means managing a constantly changing situation: into the bend, lean over, accelerate away – but with a constant shifting of weight, small twists of the accelerator, a gentle squeeze on the brake, a caress of the clutch. Do you agree?

GIACOMO If you've chosen your line properly you might have to make small adjustments but by then all the calculations have already been made. It's the same with cars: calculation, then control. On a motorcycle your eyes tend to gravitate towards the track surface more, as anything, even a small stone, can cause a fall, something which doesn't happen in a car. That makes for more tension, because even a wobble can cause a crash – and crashes hurt. In a car a mistake might cause you to spin, but then you just drive off again. There's tension in both cases, but in a car you're not worried or afraid of falling. Imagine you're taking a bend in second: the bike slips away from you, you land on your shoulder, hit your head, get hurt; in a car you press the accelerator and off you go again. In any case, whether in a car or on a motorcycle, being on the edge takes total concentration and you have to be ready to correct any wobbles or side-skids immediately.

NAO Tell me about when you won your first world championship. I can only imagine it was the biggest thrill of all.

GIACOMO I spent the night at home in Lovere, after celebrating all evening at the hotel at Arcore. Immediately after the race a huge crowd, cheering and clamouring for autographs, gathered beneath the race track building. They had even started to bend the iron fencing around the building so I moved back in the hope they would ease off. Count Agusta surprised me by saying, "It doesn't matter: today they can break what they want". Despite his strict and serious demeanour, even he knew a day of joy when he saw it. He'd chosen me because he'd wanted an Italian to ride the three-cylinder MV – and I'd done nothing less than give him the world championship. To him, it was further confirmation of the fact that he always made the right choices. He was highly ambitious, particularly in this case, because no-one had wanted the three-cylinder, only him. They'd all said the engine would be troublesome, cantankerous, impossible to ride. And he'd proved them absolutely wrong. Some thought he'd just got lucky, but when things always go right, well, I don't think luck enters into it too much: I think it means you really are smart.

NAO And the morning after the victory?

GIACOMO It was like a dream. I remember staring at all the newspapers. "Agostini World Champion", the headlines said. It was surreal. I'd always wanted to race, had started with the obstacle races and now I was *World Champion*, the planet's best. Not just the champion of Lovere or Bergamo, but the Champion of the World. It just seemed so unreal. It took me ages to realise I really was the best: perhaps I only truly realised it when I stopped, when I started watching the others race and was able to make comparisons. In many ways it was a day like any other, but it immediately put more responsibility on my shoulders because I'd become the focus of attention and the pressure was on to keep winning, for myself and the Count. It's very stressful for someone who's already won to live up to expectations: you keep having to up the ante, you're in the spotlight all the time and you mustn't disappoint anyone. As soon as things went badly or even if I finished second, you'd start hearing people say, "Agostini is finished". Honestly! Just for coming second! It really used to bug me. Still, it's better to have those sorts of responsibilities and worries than others.

NAO I think you were absolutely focussed on racing. That you were emotionally involved in nothing else, that your whole life was there, in the races. Am I wrong?

GIACOMO No. The preparation, the race, the focus on the next race: I wasn't interested in anything else. Or, rather, the race and anything to do with it came first, everything else came second.

NAO Why do champions so often get the "icicle" tag?

GIACOMO It might be that we're seen as cold because we put lives on the line, but that's unfair; it's the passion, the love of our sport that puts us out there. Of course, people sometimes see us as cold because, perhaps not even half an hour after another rider's death, off we go at 300 kph to try to win another race. But it's the wrong way of looking at things: it's not a lack of heart or sensitivity but, rather, the awareness that we've chosen to be there, that we have to carry on. Nobody wants to see misfortune strike, but we subconsciously know it can and that awareness becomes a part of you. A rider who laughs and jokes just before a race might get a reputation for being coldly detached. But what he's really feeling is unknowable. Before the start I'd always have a grin on my face, but it was just a mask that suited the occasion: deep down I was always tense, worried about winning, completing the race, getting a good start, avoiding patches of oil, not falling, not overloading the engine…

NAO Did you have a particularly low heart rate?

GIACOMO Yes, I always have done.

NAO Another reason for getting that icicle tag, then.

GIACOMO My heart rate was about the same as that of Fausto Coppi (the legendary cyclist), or thereabouts.

NAO Was it a sign of few feelings, fearlessness?

GIACOMO No, it was a sign of self control.

NAO But self control stems from the absence of fear, when you are unsurprised by things, when you control both the situation and yourself.

GIACOMO Well, I'd say that you've got self control when things happen to you and out of habit, because of your personality or a certain mental sharpness, you still manage to exert control over events. In a more private sphere, look at how people handle grief; some manifest their pain openly, wailing and crying, while others, struck by that same sense of bereavement, remain composed. Perhaps this is self control. I'm not really sure that it's the equivalent of being cold: it just might be the ability to remain lucid when terrible things happen. It means having more self control than others.

NAO Maybe this is the secret: gaining control of the situation, being aware of what's happening and what needs to be done.

GIACOMO No, it's not knowing what's happening: it's giving your all to resolve a situation.

NAO Let's take an example. A man is strolling through town one night and is attacked. If he knows how to react, what to do, if, for example he takes off his jacket and wraps it around his hand to ward off the knife, and if he knows how to throw a punch, then he'll maintain a certain calm. He is, to an extent, prepared: he has strategy and tactics. Someone else, who has no idea how to react, has never considered such a situation, will panic and lose control. The first is cold, but not the second.

GIACOMO The first considered that it could happen to him, and so he prepared for it. The second man didn't.

NAO So the champion knows what's happening and what *will* happen, and has trained accordingly. Is that what keeping a grip on things means?

GIACOMO Yes. But it's also a question of how far you're willing to think things through, anticipating all the possible scenarios; if you don't reason it out to the end you can end up looking naïve because when things happen you aren't ready to face the difficulties.

NAO Have you ever raced without really wanting to?

GIACOMO Just before the start, I reckon ninety percent of riders would be happy to pack it in.

NAO What, at the very last minute?

GIACOMO During the last getting-ready hour: by then the stress is sky-high, the commitment total and it's like having to go to work while abhorring the idea. You might yawn, feel drowsy; some would just have to go to the toilet. For instance, the German rider Martin Wimmer had to take a plastic cup to the track as he'd always have to go right at the last minute.

NAO Did you yawn?

GIACOMO Sure, plenty of us did. The tension would induce drowsiness, I'd feel worn out, exhausted and I'd be eaten away by the anxiety. Luckily, half an hour before the race I'd manage to sleep, even if it was only ten minutes. It was like pulling the plug: my battery would re-charge and I'd be off again. Perhaps it's just one of those gifts from mother nature.

NAO Who are the riders who want to race all the time?

GIACOMO The ones in the last two rows. When I waved to them at the start, I'd see them there, gathered around the motorcycle with their kids, who were laughing and mucking about. I used to think: "They don't give a damn. Here I am trembling and just look at them, chuckling and chatting". It was because I knew I had to put in a star performance while they, instead, knew they didn't stand a chance. So there was no pressure on them and they were often there just for the appearance money. Without the pressure of having to win, Count Agusta and a company counting on results there was no doubt they enjoyed themselves more than I did. They didn't have to answer to anyone; sometimes their wives doubled up as mechanics! Post-race controversy, the sort that made you out to be a has-been just because you'd finished second or third, was unknown to them. Barely a mention was given to them when the overall standings were discussed, and they'd only occasionally get a mention in the Monday newspapers. Nevertheless, there were races that I knew I couldn't win either, ones where I knew the best I could hope for was fifth or sixth place. Those were the times that I'd set off more relaxed, away from the big guns who had it in for me. It was a totally different mindset: I wasn't champing at the bit like in the other races.

NAO Has there ever been a race in which you really didn't want to participate?

GIACOMO Yes. Maybe at the Nürburgring, when it started snowing just before the start; it was absolutely freezing. It took all the fun out of it: it was no longer a race to look forward to, just a job that had to be done. There'd also be wintry days early on in the season at Salzburg in Austria: three days of rain with the leathers soaking. We'd all have preferred to pull out, but by then you were committed. When it was really cold and I still had the old soup-bowl helmet I'd spread a special cream on my forehead to keep me warm, otherwise I'd get a headache and lose my focus.

NAO How did you get on with the journalists?

GIACOMO Very well, I'd say. There weren't too many journalists assigned to motorcycling back then and, since they were so well-mannered, I made friends with just about all of them. You have to remember that journalists weren't so intent on the big scoop back then: today there's much more in-fighting than in the past. Only once was I 'scooped': Ezio Pirazzini admitted to having written that my signing fee for Yamaha was ten times higher than it really was. "What were you playing at!?", I blurted. Pirazzini was unfazed: "Giacomo, if I'd written the real figure the article wouldn't have caused a stir. With the made-up figures everyone was astonished – and what difference does it make to you anyway?", he replied. Even so, I still think it's wrong. I remember that someone, before a race at Misano, wrote that I'd passed the night with two beautiful French girls. They'd put a bottle of champagne outside my bedroom door and photographed *that*. The truth is that, yes, the girls had turned up, but I slept alone and they went back to their own rooms. I used to take things like that as a joke; I mean, after all, I was doing all right, I was winning. If things hadn't gone so well on the track Count Agusta would have had me up in front of him at Cascina Costa and asked why on earth I'd come second; and then he would have asked me to pack it in with the women, the good life and the champagne. Truth be told, I've always been a teetotaller. Luckily, things kept on going well, otherwise those articles would have damaged me.

NAO You were the first celebrity rider in the history of motorcycling and, perhaps, up until a few years ago, the *only* one too because no-one else ever achieved so much. How did that affect your private life? What happened when people in the street started recognising you, setting you up as an idol?

GIACOMO Well, it was a gradual process. People started recognising me in public in '68, '69, after I'd already won two or three world titles. A bit like Valentino Rossi, who only achieved real stardom towards 2003. The more a champion gets talked about, the more likely he is to be recognised by the man in the street, the non-fan.

NAO Did you have to attend a lot of dinners? Were there more during the lull in the season or during the race period?

GIACOMO Lots of them, yes, mostly in the non-racing period. During the race season there was very little free time: I'd go back home on Monday and be off again on Thursday. I'd decline invitations then because I wanted to be as focussed as possible. If I'd gone to those dinners I'd never have been able to turn in at ten. In the morning I used to work out, concentrate on my fitness and there's no way I'd have been able to do it. Which reminds me of an anecdote: in '64 I'd signed up with Morini and had to race in the Italian 250 Championship. Prior to a practice session at the start of the season, when I still wasn't very fit, I'd taken a holiday with friends at Alassio. Of course, being twenty-two years old, the evening before I'd gone out dancing, even though I was no hell-raiser. When I got back to Monza, two motorcycles were waiting for me. Morini's mechanic, Lambertini, was there. Anyway, I hit the track but just couldn't clock up decent times: I was missing a second a lap. I kept hacking at it, and started getting irritable. I told them I just couldn't get any more out of it: the fairing and the footrests were already scraping the tarmac and my boots had worn through to the skin as well. "You're not on form, not right", chipped in Lambertini. I felt slighted, I said it was impossible, seeing as the fairing had been so evidently smoothed by the asphalt. But Lambertini sent me home. At that point I was so disappointed I burst into tears, because the session had been cut short by my own poor performance. I honestly felt it wasn't my fault but despite being unconvinced, I started working out every morning, going to bed at half-ten and eating properly. A week later Morini booked the track at Monza again; after just six or seven laps I'd slashed a second off the previous week's times *without* touching the footrests or fairing on the floor. The bike hadn't been modified at all. It just shows what a difference preparation, the right mental approach and focus can make. Until then I'd always thought that once the bike was touching the tarmac no more could be done: instead it was good braking, the way you revved the engine that made the difference... Only your mind can let you express a potential that goes beyond your mere physical capacities.

NAO Describe a typical training day?

GIACOMO I was up at nine. I had my own personal trainer, professor Orciari, a splendid man from Pesaro. He had a gym in Bergamo and in the morning he'd come in to help me with my workout: push-ups, running, sit-ups. Towards ten-thirty I'd take the trail bike and head for the hills for an hour or so, getting back around midday. Then I had a shower. I'd have lunch at one and be free in the afternoon. I did what most men my age did: and that largely consisted of chasing women. I did my duty in the morning and let off steam in the afternoon. I'd be in bed by ten-thirty, eleven at the latest. I ate well and never drank or smoked. That was how it was from Monday to Thursday. Then, prior to the race, I stopped training because I didn't want to expend any more energy: it would be needed on the track during the qualifying on Friday and Saturday and then in the race itself on Sunday. Of course, by the time the race season came round I was pretty fit anyway. Other riders would run ten kilometres the morning before the race while I just took it easy with a massage. Too much practice on the bike could be counterproductive too. It was better to make frequent pit stops and weed out mechanical imperfections, or suspend the practice session to take a rest. If you squeeze yourself dry, you just end up being out of juice at the crucial moment. Later on, my experience as team manager, with Kenny Roberts for instance, confirmed this was the right approach. When we had a practice session, Roberts would achieve record-breaking times on the first day and then slow down a bit on the second; the third day he slowed further. It's just unreasonable to expect a rider to practice ten days straight and turn in stunning performances every single day. Whenever I went to Japan for a fortnight to test the Yamaha I had a well-defined track schedule: from ten to midday and from two to four in the afternoon. Then I'd relax, get a massage and some light exercise, a sauna, a good meal and be in bed at eleven and up again the next morning. It was a schedule designed to keep you relaxed. The track was booked for me all day long, but I only made use of it four hours a day.

NAO Did you read books, go to the cinema?

GIACOMO I wasn't a keen reader. I'd flit from one thing to another, from a booklet to a magazine. I'd prefer to play tennis, go cycling, take a walk or do a spot of skiing. Whenever I got some free time I'd never dedicate myself to any one thing and master it; I'd try my hand at everything, a bit superficially perhaps, because, in any case, my real passion was motorcycling. For example, in Helsinki I once found this huge DIY store, the sort that didn't yet exist in Italy, and I spent hours looking at all these tools, buying up wrenches and hammers that I couldn't get hold of at home. In Japan, instead, I'd lose myself in their marvellous department stores, and then the day after maybe I'd visit the waterfalls, go sailing or hiking, play tennis. After two or three days I'd be back in the department store, which I found fascinating. I've always loved seeing and doing a bit of everything.

NAO Going back to racing, Phil Read's arrival at MV seems a little odd because you'd enjoyed absolute dominion from 1966 to 1972. Why was he taken on?

GIACOMO Because MV didn't want to run the risk of me resting on my laurels, they wanted to keep the pressure on by giving me an adversary. If I said "The bike's not right", they wanted to be able to say, "Yes it is, 'cause Phil wins on it". And if I kept winning they'd be able to say to him, "If Agostini can win, then so must you". You were always being pushed.

NAO But it had never happened previously.

GIACOMO Well, at the start of things there was Hailwood.

NAO Sure, but after that, for seven years, you were without a high-calibre team-mate.

GIACOMO Well, I did have Bergamonti and Pagani. In any case, maybe Read's arrival had something to do with the fact that the new four-cylinder was on its way, something I wasn't too happy about: I was of the opinion that the engine wasn't much good. This got some people's backs up at MV. We argued, and I said I didn't want to test it. Read, instead, said the bike would be fantastic with this engine, and they loved him for it. So I said, "Fine, let Read test it". I picked him up from Linate airport at ten in the morning. He was on the track by eleven. At one in the afternoon he was back at Linate, waiting for a plane to whisk him home: he'd managed just three laps before the bike broke down irreparably. He'd correctly calculated that if he told them they were right he'd get a warm welcome. But I was only interested in telling the truth, because if you really want to make a contribution to removing the defects from a motorcycle and make some real headway then you just have to be frank. At that time I was saying the engine was heavy, under-performing, skittish and generally problematic. Later, at the 1973 race at Hockenheim, a fast circuit where you need power, I asked for the 4-cylinder 500 because I thought, on that particular track, I'd be able to coax some success out of it. Out of spite, they didn't let me have it. By then of course, they'd made improvements and I had more faith in it. I hadn't said I would *never* test it, I'd said a lot of work needed to be done to get it right. Read, in the meantime, had had a son and named him Rocky, just like Agusta's son (Agusta was then team manager). They got on extremely well, which would have been fine by me if things had gone the way I'd wanted them to, that is, if we'd all been sincere and spoken openly about the pros and cons of the bike. But that's not the way it went. Let's say internal team politics took hold – something I've always found distasteful. It riled me a bit. In '74, with Yamaha, I'd have won both titles - the 350 and the 500 - immediately if I hadn't injured my shoulder and it would have been sweet revenge. However, after two years with Yamaha, which withdrew from racing at the end of '75, I competed on an MV again in my own self-managed team, alternating with the Suzuki in the 500. In '76 the engine broke down, otherwise it would have been another title in 350. In '77, instead, I had a Yamaha in the 500 and 750 categories.

NAO During these last two years of your motorcycling career you were the champion of champions, but by then a generation away from up-and-coming youngsters who were starting to make a name for themselves, such as Barry Sheene.

GIACOMO No. Sheene competed against me for a long time; he started winning when I was on my way out, when I did my last year as an independent. I had wanted to retire, because MV had left the scene and so had Yamaha: instead I continued for another two years.

NAO Was the MV still competitive in 1976?

GIACOMO At low revs, it performed better than the two-strokes. I chose it for the Nürburgring race because, when it rained, the MV four-stroke was smoother to handle. Just a few minutes before the race

I managed, by sleight of hand, to replace the Suzuki - which had a habit of seizing - with the MV. The Suzuki was a disappointment: it had a great frame and 130 HP as opposed to the MV's 110 HP. On a good day it was outstanding. But it was hard to squeeze all the power out of it and when you did manage it you'd do three laps and the engine would seize. You'd be flying, then suddenly you'd be parking. All in all, a negative experience, even though, like I said, it was a joy to ride and when the engine was working well it was working brilliantly: you really felt like you were soaring.

NAO These last two years are rather marginal to your career.

GIACOMO Yes. I knew the end was nigh. I wasn't as motivated as I used to be, I'd won just about everything. I'd already thought about packing it in the year before but I still wanted another go at it. In the end, all the little problems made me decide that it was time to hang up the helmet.

NAO What did you think of the up-and-coming youngsters?

GIACOMO In this game, beyond the age of thirty-two, you're already on a downhill slide. When you're younger you don't worry, you're more reckless, accidents don't exist: the older you get, though, the more you use your head, and that means more thoughts. People think we're mad, but that's not how it is. Madmen do not win. Being young gives you one clear advantage: you're better at *not* thinking. That was pretty damned useful in my day, when the tracks were so dangerous it would give you the creeps just to look at them. Recently I saw some footage of a Tourist Trophy, and remembering what I'd seen on that circuit, I told *myself* I must have been mad. But that was the track, it was where we had to race and we simply had to make the best of it. It was the same with peasants who always had nothing to eat except polenta and cheese: if you asked them what it was like they'd tell you it was good.

The Winner's masterpiece, considered Nao, was not winning fifteen world titles but succeeding in becoming Giacomo Agostini. That was his achievement. Everything else was a consequence of it: the victories, the success, the money, the women, the dream family.

Remaining competitive had always been part of the game and the game would never end.

For example, Agostini had insisted on a certain photo for the cover, one that showed him on the starting grid, a plaster on his nose, just like today's riders, thirty-five years on.

"The plaster... just like Valentino Rossi. You don't want to be second to anyone, do you?", Nao had said to him.

"Good man. I see you're beginning to understand", Ago had replied.

Nao had watched some video tapes that Agostini had given him.

For the very first time, he'd watched him race. And he was fascinated: while the bikes did seem to be going more slowly than they do today and the camera angles weren't quite as thrilling, there was still a strong impression of speed and – with those skinny, feeble-looking tyres – risk. Watching these men guide their motorcycles through the bends gave an impression of lightness and freedom; a little sentimentalising was, thought Nao, inevitable in these cases. It was almost as if they were dancing through the curves, in an unstable equilibrium requiring constant correction. The bike tilted this way then that, the rider shifting his weight on the saddle, the front wheel sinking forward as they braked, the rear wheel being driven down as they accelerated away: more than a display of strength, it was an exhibition of coordination, agility and fast reflexes.

The films were of the Tourist Trophy on the Isle of Man – the 1967 edition no less – the one that Ago had called the race of his life.

He wore rectangular goggles, the soup-bowl helmet, a yellow T-shirt beneath the thin leather suit. His steed was the three-cylinder MV 500. His race number was nine.

Before the start, a gaggle of girls gathered round him to get their autographs. Smiling away, he radiated calm: he made it all look so easy, like when he dismounted from the 350 and a few minutes later was ready for the start of the 500.

At the start Hailwood went first, then Agostini.

Hailwood had lost his suit number so he started off with the number four on the bike and number one on the suit.

At a certain point on the course – Nao couldn't remember what it was – the accompanying commentary had said that speeds of 260 kph were achieved. Average speeds were around 170. People would lean out from their balconies to watch the riders whiz by.

No Italian had ever won the 500 cc race, the Senior TT. It was a superb opportunity for Agostini, as he'd made his debut in TT just two years before.

Hailwood's Honda was powerful but harder to handle on the bends, Agostini's MV less powerful but more agile.

They'd flew like lightning bolts. First one had the upper hand, then the other, the gap never being more than a few seconds. At a certain point the gap dropped to three seconds, in Agostini's favour.

Until then, no-one had ever stretched Hailwood so far.

It was 16th June 1967. Agostini's twenty-fifth birthday.

At the Ramsey they'd both touched the roadside hay bales: then Agostini's chain broke – and Hailwood won.

Nao restarted the tape.

NAO Tell me more about the Tourist Trophy? What was it like to race there?

GIACOMO Riders were started off at ten-second intervals, in pairs. Quarter Bridge was the first obstacle. After the start there was this long downhill section, a sort of dip, which could be really dangerous because when you went at full throttle with a full load of oil and petrol the sump would thump against the tarmac: you'd throttle back a bit there. Then you'd come to Quarter Bridge, where the fastest part of the course began, from Braddan Bridge to Elm Bank, from The Highlander to Ballacraine Corner, the fastest point of the lot. The asphalt there was excellent, there was just this big jump to do on an uphill section where you could reach 280 kph. As soon as you reached the top of the rise the bike would nose up so you had to get ready for the jump by shifting your weight forwards to keep the front wheel on the ground. You'd close down the gas just a fraction and get your weight as far forwards as possible to maximise adhesion, because as soon as the skip was over you were back to full throttle. The Highlander was a long false straight with wide, sweeping bends; but among these were hidden second-gear bends. That was the worst thing about the TT, because you'd arrive at 280 kph and had to remember exactly where a certain second gear chicane was. You had to be alert every inch of the way. Then you'd come to Ballacraine Corner, taken in second or first depending on the motorcycle, and the western, return side of the circuit would begin. There was Doran's Bend, Laurel Bank and Glen Helen where I fell in '66. For me, that was where things started getting tricky: a mixed. fast section followed, with lots of blind corners. You carried on to Handley's Corner, then Ballaugh Bridge, which became famous because everyone would jump there, making it look like a motocross event: it was spectacular, but not particularly difficult or dangerous because it was done in second gear. After Ballaugh Bridge things just got harder: you carried on to Ginger Hall, where there was a difficult tract that you just had to know by heart. A straight then took you to the Hairpin and the tight, narrow Ramsey bend. That was where the flats finished and you headed up into the hills. At Bungalow you went over the railway. The hills were insidious, because sometimes there'd be fog or rain. It was extremely difficult: you'd start off in the sun and have no idea what it would be like later on. In theory the hills would let you move at 250-260 kph or more, but you might have to drop to 80 because of the fog and follow the white line in the middle of the road – and the road was just four metres wide. From Bungalow you began the descent back to Douglas. That section of the TT left me with some bad memories, because it was on one of those bends, Hailwood Rise I think, that Parlotti fell and was killed. Then you dropped down to Creg-ny-Baa, where, in '67, the chain on my 500 snapped when I was in the lead. Just before the finish there was a sharp, first gear bend. It was Governor's Bridge, where they'd divert you off the road and slip you in between two boulders where there was always damp and moss on the ground. After that little bend you'd breathe a sigh of relief because you knew you were nearly there. Information on the time gaps was given to me at Sulby Straight: because the circuit was so long I couldn't wait until I went past the pits to get my info. That would have meant an update only once every nineteen or twenty minutes. So they'd let me know the situation when I was half-way round and at the finish. A board with the gap in seconds, accompanied by a plus or minus sign, was held up. I have some bizarre memories of the TT. For instance, at Ballaugh Bridge, every year, even if it was five in the morning, there would be a woman in a long dress standing on her doorstep. Every time I went by she'd raise her dress a little in a curtsy and wave to me. One day, while I was out practicing, I decided to stop and say hello to her: this dame who waved to Agostini every day, every lap had become something of a legend. The race lasted six laps, totalling 360 kilometres. After the third lap we stopped to refuel, oil the chain, see if the tyres needed changing and top up the supplementary oil tank under the saddle.

A rider, thought Nao, is a man who lives to a schedule, a set of programmed challenges. The rhythm of his life is dictated by the race calendar, just as time is dictated by hours. He wandered whether this was a good thing or not, if a life like that could be fun and easy-going, whether there might be a risk of it getting monotonous. No, he thought, it was probably a great life: you knew the day and the time that you would have to give it your all.

The Winner no longer rode motorcycles. he only did so if they asked him to take a spin on the track at some special event. He did it, but rather reluctantly it seemed. He wasn't one of those ex-pros who stays in the saddle to the very end. Yet there had been days when he'd flown as high as a kite on a motorcycle, days in which not only had he been the world's best, but also the world's fastest.

Nao remembered an anecdote that Agostini had recounted. He'd shown him a painting depicting him neck and neck with Hailwood at the Sachsenring in '67. "It was incredible", he'd said, "we were racing *alongside* each other. We were so close that when we exited that bend at the end, see it? It looked like there was one bike only: my mechanics fretted because they thought one of us had fallen and feared it might be me".

Nao lifted his gaze from the table and knocked over some stupid soft toy he'd received as a free gift on one of his trips abroad. He had no idea why he'd kept it. He kept everything else he was given too.

Looking at that stupid soft toy, he thought about presents. He never gave presents. He only did so at Christmas or on birthdays – and only if he got an invite to a party. Above all, Nao never brought presents back from his trips abroad. He didn't bring his parents any, or his friends – or his girlfriend, when he had one. In fact, he hated people who brought him presents, those "little somethings" as they called them, from their business trips. If you're on a business trip then you shouldn't have time to be worrying about "little somethings". And if you're a professional in your field you don't waste time on browsing trinkets, stuff so insignificant that's forgotten as soon as it's unwrapped, or reluctantly-eaten foods (such as the pastries that Nao hated but were one of the most common gifts going). No, Nao wasn't the least bit interested in giving gifts to make the 'right' impression, just to show that he'd remembered this person or that. And he didn't want to be ripped off either: because when you buy something in an unknown place to which you are unlikely to return (the wily salesman recognises the one-time traveller instantly – and the world's full of wily salesmen), you will be mathematically taken to the cleaner's. And Nao wasn't too keen on that at all.

Tape n° 5
The need to make choices

Nao drove through the evening, his thoughts gravitating towards Agostini.

Drifting through the neon-lit night-city, he admired the bright billboards - so different from their daytime counterparts - that seemed to airbrush the landscape. He was especially fond of the wide avenues where the traffic was hastier: here there were no shop fronts, just lines of barrack-like buildings and the central reservation. Driving slowly, he observed his surroundings. Ever since he was a child he'd counted lampposts during car journeys. During never-ending trips with his father and the rest of his family to holiday destinations, or Sunday visits to aunts and uncles, he used to kill time by counting the lampposts or, if they were on the motorway, road signs or guardrail uprights. Even now, as he drove around the city, he counted the lampposts until something else captured his gaze. Afterwards he'd start again, as if nothing has happened, as if everything was reset at that instant.

However, Nao, while he was out that evening, couldn't help but think of the Winner. Images, rather than actual thoughts, popped into his brain. His mind was obviously going to work on the Agostini story and the process of productive fermentation was under way.

He could seen him sitting, just as he had one day, in shirt sleeves, arms crossed, tie draped over a forearm to stop it getting creased.

He could see him eating a cutlet with his hands in Milan's best hotel, devouring it with the appetite of the hungry. He'd just finished a celebrity appearance and as he'd chewed his eyes had trailed the supple form of a model as she swayed past him.

He saw him wandering around his home in a pair of worn slippers, his gait characterised by the short, quick steps that Nao had come to recognise as an Agostini trademark. It reminded Nao of the way squirrels moved – or at least one he'd once seen on TV.

Apart from being a god of motorcycling, what was so special about this man, Nao asked himself?

Yes, what made 'Ago' so special?

Nao reflected for a moment, then came to the conclusion that the great thing about Ago was that he was a powerhouse, had an iron will, was able to cultivate the qualities that would make him Number One and ensure he stayed a winner, a man of success for the rest of his life. In short, he had balls.

"But", Nao then asked himself, "what does it mean to have balls?".

It was one of those questions that could drive you mad. Perhaps one of those questions it was best you never asked yourself. He instinctively slowed, pulled over, cut the engine and stared intro space.

No, he shouldn't have asked himself that question.

He struggled for the right thought, the answer. He turned the question over in his mind two or three times. The answer didn't come. "I don't know", thought Nao. "No, right now, I just do not know what it means to have balls".

He decided not to think about it any more. At least not for the time being.

The fact that it had been a bit strange for an answer to elude him didn't cross his mind either. Usually he had an answer for everything, even if it was only a banal one. Was he refusing the question?

He went home, settled down and got back to work.

He pressed 'Play' and was once again in the company of Giacomo Agostini.

NAO One of your most famous performances was at the Daytona 200 in 1974. How did things go?

GIACOMO Well, I've been back to Daytona this year to celebrate the 30th anniversary of that victory, my first with Yamaha. Daytona is always an exhilarating race. This year it attracted 550 thousand motorcyclists. Imagine it: a Grand Prix sometimes only draws 30 thousand. Unfortunately they're people who go there to show off with their own motorcycles. Some even have their bikes 'chauffeured' there; they then fly in to find their Harley-Davidson ready and waiting. There are shops there where you can buy anything, where you can have your motorcycle painted any way you like: just leave it there for an hour or two and, like true artists, they'll paint your fuel tank, top box etc. just as you see fit. There's a 500-square-metre shop where you can get everything for your Harley-Davidson: special footrests, steel rims, custom-made spare parts. I even saw a skull that lights up when you brake. One evening we were at a restaurant and there was a bike that lit up like a Christmas tree: it had coloured lights everywhere to highlight the braking system, the chain and every other part of the bike. It was beautiful. There are people who work for years so they can afford the bike of their dreams, spending anything up to a hundred thousand dollars. Seeing the oval where I won back in '74 was an extremely pleasant experience.

NAO What did it make you think?

GIACOMO Firstly, it made me realise that I'm getting old and that I'll never be able to race there again. There's always a touch of melancholy when I go along to these events, because I can't help but think of the sheer joy these places have given me. I cried when I won at Daytona. Knowing that I won't ever be able to do these things again always saddens me a bit. But then I tell myself you just have to be intelligent about it and understand that the way has to be left open for others.

NAO Understandable, but you're still a protagonist at these events, still the centre of attention.

GIACOMO Yamaha organised a party to celebrate the thirtieth anniversary of my victory: Eddie Lawson, Wayne Rainey, Steve Baker and lots of others were there. We also did some autograph sessions, the way they do in America: two hours one day, two hours another. All these Americans queuing up, book in hand, to get an autograph...

NAO Is it fair to say that you've always remained the rider, the champion? Is it also fair to say that you're somewhat a prisoner, a slave to this character? I think so.

GIACOMO Well, since I didn't enter into this career out of chance but because I wanted to at any cost, I still get excited when I watch a race, this beautiful show on two wheels. It was at Daytona, in fact, that I was able to admire a 19-year-old kid putting in an incredible show of acrobatics on his bike. He flies up in the air, lets go of the bike and flips round: when he trains he uses a huge swimming pool full of water and foam rubber as a crash mat. The first time he tried that jump he broke an arm, a shoulder and three or four ribs. Seeing him fly ten or twelve metres off the ground, let go of the handlebars and the bike, flip round, grab the handlebars again and sit back on the bike is breathtaking. It's all down to endless training: he sent shivers down the spine – mine and my motocross friends' too.

Nao switched off the tape player.

"He didn't answer my question", he thought. But then again, there wasn't much to say: it was thus, he was the prisoner of his own person. It was just that he couldn't – or wouldn't - see it. He focussed on living, doing, travelling continuously and keeping himself terribly busy. That was why he hadn't answered the question: he simply wasn't able to ask himself whether his own life had been anything other than the fast, winning ride it had been and continued to be because, for him, it was simply impossible for it to be anything else.

It dawned on Nao that, as co-writer of Agostini's biography, a little success might come his way too. 'Ago' was virtually a guarantee of success, of victory: it was probably contagious. Yes, contagious, thought Nao.

NAO Tell me about the Daytona race.

GIACOMO It was 1974, my first race with a two-stroke, my first race in America and my first race with Yamaha. Daytona is one of those circuits with raised, banked bends. It's exiting those bends that's the trickiest part: here, the centrifugal force pushes you up against the wall. I was extremely tense. Practice consisted of one fast lap and Kenny Roberts had done it half a second faster than me. I knew winning it would be a tough proposition, because Roberts had already competed there many times. He had these special tyres: they were very wide and made changes of direction difficult, but they stuck to the asphalt like glue, which was perfect when you're spending so much time on long sweeping bends. I tried them myself, but without any prior experience I just couldn't ride properly. At the start I went into it head-down. On the first fast lap, with the tank full, I established a new track record, then I had to battle it out with Kenny Roberts. He got a little tight and I took the lead. It was a scorching hot day, a staggering forty-five degrees Celsius and it was a long race. I was used to races of less than half that distance: in a Grand Prix we would do 120, 130 kilometres, but at Daytona we had to cover 360. It was taxing because you had to stop twice to refuel and change the tyres. Yet there I was, in the lead in my very first race: it was unreal, I was a first-timer in every way possible, the race was legendary, and I was winning it. It was also the first time the stands had been filled to capacity: there must have been seventy or eighty thousand people. People had flown in from Italy, France Britain and Holland. My own participation in the race probably drew a lot of people too. At the half-way mark I was already dehydrated because, as a habit, I never drank before a race. I didn't think I'd be able to make it, I wanted to stop. I was doing 300 kph and dreaming of being in the hotel pool, swimming underwater with my mouth wide open. Sweat ran down into my eyes, I couldn't spit. I was desperate. I kept wanting to stop. Then I thought of all those people who had made such an effort to come and see me and my pride kicked in where my body couldn't. I realised that an opportunity like this comes but once. I scraped the bottom of the barrel, pumped myself up mentally - and it worked because just one minute later I felt the desperation and stress ebbing away. I'd come through 'the wall'. I finished the race - and finished it first. Once I took the chequered flag I no longer had the strength to grip the handlebars. My concentration evaporated and I collapsed into my friends' arms. Seeing the state I was in, one of them began to cry. I was so dehydrated they set up a drip feed and later on, at the prize ceremony, I went up on the stage for just a moment and then went straight back to the hotel room, the doctor in close attendance. I lost three kilos during the race: I was already thin, but I now looked emaciated: it was difficult to look at myself in the mirror. My hands were covered in blisters which started coming off and bleeding. But I was overjoyed, because I'd won a race that meant so much to me. I'd left MV, moved to Yamaha: a lot of people were sure I wouldn't be able to win without the MV, but I proved them wrong. Like I said, it was unreal.

NAO Was that your only race at Daytona?

GIACOMO No. In 1975 I took part in the 200 Mile again. I prepared for it this time, had Dr. Costa come with me: he had me eat, together with my usual cappuccino, some horrible-tasting jams that gave me everything I would need during the race: mineral salts and other stuff to give me energy. Yet I only managed to finish fourth because the engine had problems right from the start and grumbled throughout the race. There wasn't the heat of the previous year: 1974 proved to be a fluke and it's never been so hot at Daytona since. I prepared for it meticulously, but given the cooler weather it seemed like I'd ridden an altogether different race. If it hadn't been for the mechanical problems I'm sure I'd have won; instead, destiny decided that I should win the first time, when I wasn't ready for it and in the middle of an extraordinary heat wave.

Yes, destiny. If you want something too intensely, thought Nao, it'll stay out of your reach. He wasn't sure why, but that's how it was. Instead, if you're not too bothered, great and beautiful things might happen and you'll appreciate them all the more when they do. It's the same with women, mused Nao: the more you like one, the less you should think about her. If it's destiny, it'll happen anyway, otherwise there's nothing to be done. It's all so simple really: it's us who complicate our lives with useless worries.

NAO When did you decide to get married?

GIACOMO I believed a career in motorcycling to be incompatible with having a family: there was too much danger, too much being away. I just couldn't have travelled the world, risked my life *and* been married. So I tried to put marriage out of my mind. It was when I stopped, at forty, and became a team manager that I started thinking about it. One day Marlboro organised a press conference at Jerez, in Spain. I was there to present the team, which then included Eddie Lawson. Some Spanish models and interpreters were also there, one of whom was particularly good looking. I asked the event organiser for her name and he told me she was called Maria. In the evening we had to go to Seville for a TV programme, and I really didn't feel like it. So I said I'd only go if the girl came along. So it was. She was an interpreter. And a delightful person. We went out to dinner and when we said goodbye I told her I'd be back in a month and a half or so for the Spanish GP. It was the team's first time there so I asked her if she wouldn't mind finding some apartments for the mechanics as the hotels were fully booked. We kept in touch by phone, her to keep me up to speed, me to listen to her voice: the whole thing was just an excuse to talk to her. When I came back for the Grand Prix we started seeing each other a bit more. She had found some apartments in a residential hotel, she came along to the practice sessions, then the restaurant and it was there that a solid attraction took hold. However, four or five days later I had to leave. We stayed in touch and one day, while I was heading to Germany for a Grand Prix, I decided to go and see her. "I'm passing through anyway", I said. It was easy enough… we had our own aeroplane and I went to see her several times before gradually establishing a relationship with her. It dawned on me that I'd found the right woman and decided to marry. It was a tough decision for me because I'd always refused the idea: but looking ahead I realised my career was no longer as dangerous as it had been and I'd have more time to dedicate to the family, so we got married. The wedding was wonderful. As a present Marlboro sent a film crew to record the ceremony. Yamaha sent me a motorcycle, and when I left the church I got on it with Maria and rode to her home for the reception. She'd arrived in a carriage drawn by ten white horses, my mother in a carriage with ten chestnut horses. My relatives and friends from Italy, 140-150 of them, flew in on my plane. My parents found everything rather odd, let's say, but over there it doesn't matter who you are, all weddings are pompous affairs, very different from ours... For instance, Ave Maria played and sung in flamenco style gives you goose bumps. When, two days later, I left Spain with my wife, I realised I was taking her away from her country, from Andalusia, and I felt guilty about it: for love she was willing to leave her country, family, her seven brothers and sisters. As the plane took off I could see in her eyes that it had been a tough choice for her, whether it was for love or not. Luckily, we had two children, a girl, now fifteen years old, and a boy, now nine and she no longer feels so far away, even if she does love her Andalusia, loves to return to the warmth of the Costa del Sol. We often go there. It's a great place and all the friends I've ever invited there have had a great time. Food's great, people aren't nosy. Andalusians always say "Mañana", aren't clock-watchers like the Italians. We once had an appointment with a solicitor and the people with me had forgotten the documents. If it had happened here the solicitor would have gone ballistic; instead he just took us along to a café for a drink and those delicious Andalusian snacks, the tapite. I then asked him when we should come back and he just said "Mañana, evening time". In Bergamo the solicitor would have made us wait another month, and been pretty grouchy with it too.

NAO Was it more a case of the right woman or the right time?

GIACOMO Both. I was forty-five years old, it was time. But Maria was right too, because I didn't just fall in love with her: I fell in love with her entire family. They're great, very close to each other, whenever we go to Spain with just our closest relatives there are twenty-five of us at the table. Maria, the youngest sister, has six children alone. Of course, you also need to have the means to maintain a family of that size... With Maria I closed the door on the playboy period, which was largely fiction anyway. I reckon that's how it should be, how life should be lived. If you get married young, it's all over: by the time you're twenty-five you've done everything you're ever going to do. Instead, you have to gain experience, build up your career, *then* meet your companion and enjoy life with her, then have children and enjoy life with them. I think life's good when it's divided into periods. It's like sitting down to a good meal: if you scoff everything at once you only end up with indigestion, yet if you take time to taste the starter, the main course and so on, it will be memorable…

The tape finished right there with those words. His summary of life had been clichéd, crude even, expressed with a metaphor of utter simplicity. But Nao thought there were two things in life: there's life itself and there are words, and only the former counts. Agostini was interested in life, not the words to describe it. Those that dwell on words do so because they find it hard to get a life or they aren't strong enough to make the most of life and so fail and seek refuge in words. People to be avoided, mused Nao, despite the fact that his own livelihood was carved out of words. But he was raw - shabby even, if he was willing to be honest - and his life was real for the precise reason that it was so banal, so anchored to reality, to things, small-scale power play, success and defeat. Just like Ago, he wasn't one to beat about the bush. Even his writing was to the point: just a few concepts, clearly explained. His pieces would open with an ordinariness that was surprising, but that was the beauty of them. It was him all over: solid, never-changing, predictable but reliable, ambitious and therefore obedient. No mincing, no high-minded concepts. Trivial one-liners and a touch of coarseness, more likely. You immediately knew where he was at, both in work and in life. He offered up his good points and bad points immediately, and his limitations were visible a mile off. He didn't try to exploit imagination, creativity or any other qualities that weren't his. He offered himself up for what he was, and that was what made him a man.

Women. What Nao wanted, in the end, was to be chosen by a woman. He had never asked himself what qualities or reasons a woman would base such a choice on or why she should end up choosing him. Yet his main reason for wandering about it was that he had a high opinion of himself, believed himself to be full of qualities. If he were *chosen* by a woman he would simply see if she fitted the bill and, if she did, well, he'd stick with her. This was the truth at the core of Nao's mind. Searching for the right woman and winning her heart wasn't for him. In any case, his courting technique would have been second-rate. No, she would just have to recognise Nao's qualities and abandon herself to him, but without getting too heavy. Nao knew the score by now: marriage was marriage, it wasn't fun.

He'd learnt this from a man he'd once met in a bar, a former pimp who'd retired and married a woman of wealth. Now over sixty, he enjoyed the good life - with *her* money. Every now and again he'd come into the bar, elegantly dressed with his hair smoothed back, dark glasses rimming his eyes, even at night. Hard as nails he was: it made you uneasy just to look at him. This was someone who'd seen action, and plenty of it. He'd served time for some of those actions too. Nao, was drawn to him immediately as he couldn't help but like such characters. Since Nao was, physically at least, anything but imposing, he didn't instil any fear. In fact, he had a way of making you talk and tell, even confide in him - even hardened criminals, inasmuch as such men do any confiding. Nevertheless, this former pimp had opened up and started talking about women. Nao had asked him what he'd learnt about them and he said they'd been his lifelong passion, despite his utter conviction that they *cannot* be understood. There was no point in speaking with them because they were purely instinctive and were only happy when men stimulated that instinctiveness; if you tried to get them to think and decide, carry on alone, they either felt lost or faded. Women, he had gone on to say, should be loved - and sometimes beaten, because they then feel even more loved. That, he had said, is why we are all animals: because after a good beating we're all happier. Not everyone, he'd continued, knows how to love women: loving them means dedicating yourself to them, making them happy, even if it means you have to do things that are totally incomprehensible. At that point Nao had asked him whether he thought love existed or not. And the man had said that it didn't. There is, rather, a point in a man's life in which he feels it's time to start a family. So he no longer looks for a woman to have a good time with, to have great sex with, but a woman he can marry and have children with. And he needs to be alert, because finding the right woman is no easy task. You need to like her but not be infatuated with her, because the happiness you'll have with her will not be young love's joy or the complicity of an affair but the conscious happiness of the man who has made the right choice.

Nao only reflected on his own life at night. No particular thoughts crossed his mind, perhaps he just felt a touch lonely, that was all. In the final analysis he rather agreed with the ex-pimp, who saw things in much the same way as Agostini did. First a man has to enjoy himself and when he matures and knows what to do he chooses a woman to settle down and have a family with. Yes, it's what he would do too. Because there are two types of men in this world: those who take people for a ride and those that get taken for a ride. And he knew perfectly well which group he wanted to belong to.

He turned in for the night, feeling self-satisfied. Satisfied with the work he'd done, because the day was over and he'd taken another step forward, because he liked his life as it was, even if - or perhaps because - there was as yet no woman in it. This life as a confirmed bachelor, a stray dog, suited him: he'd often told himself so. And even though he was incapable of giving, to a woman or anyone else, it wasn't a problem for the simple reason that he was totally unaware of it and thus thought that all was right, that everything was going splendidly.

Before falling asleep his mind returned to the question that had occurred to him in the car. Yes: what does it mean to have balls?
Does it mean toughing it out to the bitter end?
Finding the courage to do things you'd rather not?
Making the right choices?
Taking your own path, being yourself?
Knowing when to step down?
Knowing how to apologise?
Knowing how to forgive?
Not giving a damn about others?
Being patient?
Not being afraid of yourself?

Incredibly he just couldn't answer that question. It annoyed him. It just wasn't possible for him not to come up with anything, anything at all.

Such was his irritation he decided to give it no more thought. But he was certain of one thing: Agostini had balls.

And Nao? It was too soon to say, he was too young, he hadn't yet demonstrated anything.

Without really knowing why, Nao asked himself this question: "What action would Agostini be willing to take if someone tried to take away his wife, Maria?". He thought that anyone who crossed him would get hurt, very seriously hurt. You could see he was tough. You could feel it.

Nao, instead, had no woman to fight for. He had a job in which he was essentially just a go-between and his laconic manner meant that he never took any position particularly seriously. If people got his back up he'd get irate, but it was largely an act. He had nothing which he could really call his own, nothing worth risking everything for: that was his weakness.

Once, while he was being driven back to the station after one of their interviews, Agostini's mobile had rung. As the conversation progressed he began to anger and started raising his voice. At the end he turned to Nao, even though he was really talking to himself, and blurted "Honestly, why does everything always have to end in argument?". The problem was that a construction company was completing a new building for him and he wasn't happy with how they were getting on. Agostini had blocked the payments.

"And if he should argue with me one day?", thought Nao.

Despite this last thought he still fell asleep almost instantly, as peacefully as always.

Of his capacity to doze off easily and sleep soundly, he always said "It's because I sleep the sleep of the just".

Winning motorcycle races takes talent and shrewdness. In this picture a bright-eyed Agostini seems to ooze both.

The king (of motorcycling) enjoys himself on horseback: here he dominates a thoroughbred in the hills near his birthplace.

Ago jokingly poses for photographers in the car of a well-known Italo-Belgian painter with whom he always used to stay during the Belgian GP at Spa-Francorchamps.

Above: after winning everything in the World Motorcycling Championships,
in 1974 he went on to claim the Daytona 200 title.
Below: his 1975 return to the US brought little success.

Ago in tears after winning the Daytona 200 in 1974 on a Yamaha 700: the scorching weather has left him totally dehydrated.

At his villa in the hills near Bergamo. Rather than setting up the classic basement taverna, Agostini kitted it out with a gym to keep himself in tip-top shape. Below: the lounge.

Above: pleased parents display a blow-up photo of sons Giacomo and Felice in a motocross event. Below: Ago poses proudly in front of his just-completed villa.

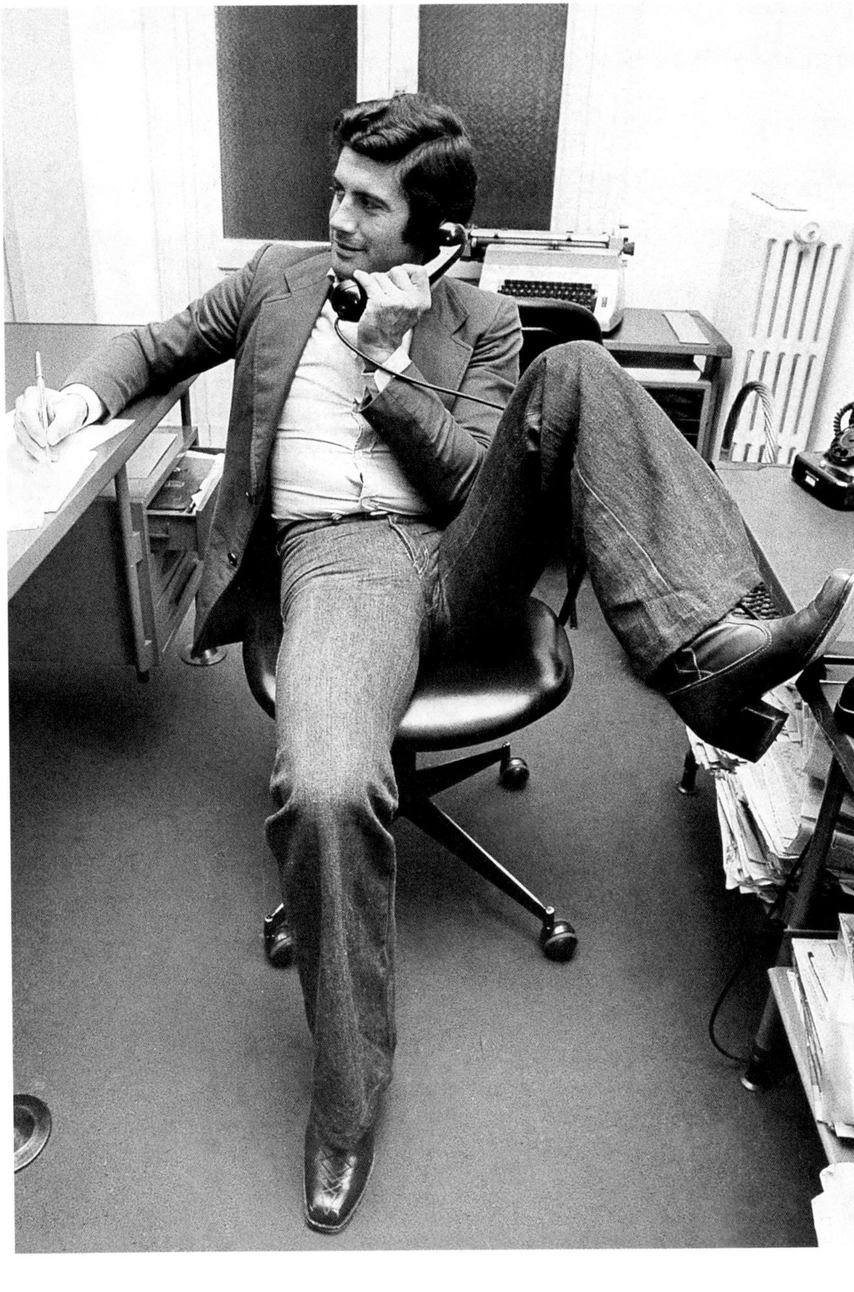

Giacomo Agostini was one of the first to make the step from track racer
to self-manager, thus taking on board a host of non-motorcycling commitments.

Idolised by the crowds, adored by women: with his magnetic Latin charm, he even managed to win the hearts of those with no real interest in the sport.

1971: pictured with Giuseppe Saragat, Giacomo Agostini is made a Knight of the Republic.

The Seventies saw champions starting to endorse products.
Agostini was one of the first riders to embrace this new role.

1978: the four-wheeled chapter of Giacomo Agostini's life unfolds.
Driving a Chevron in Formula 2 during the European Championship.

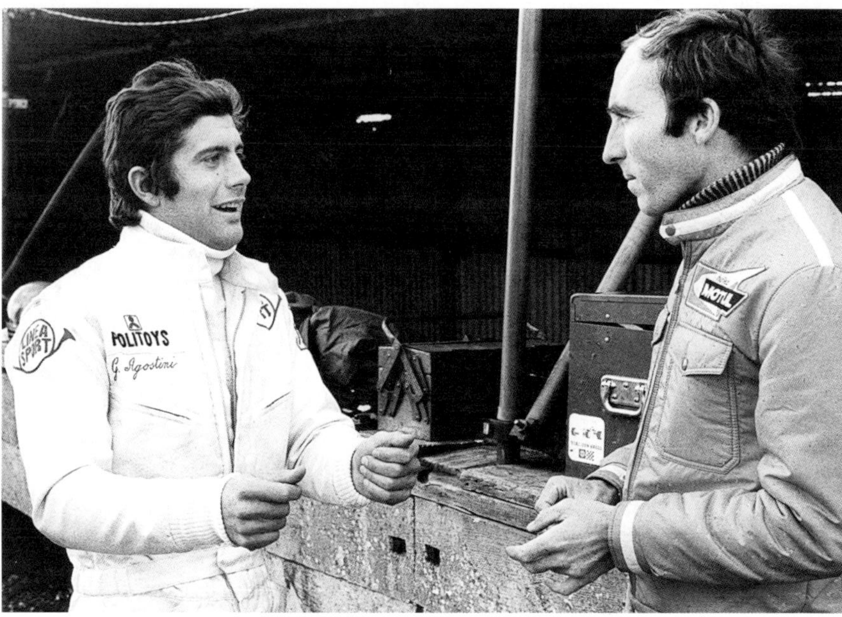

Above: in 1979. taking part in the Aurora Championship with a Williams Formula 1.
Below: Ago gives Frank Williams valuable feedback on the car's performance.

Hat-trick of champions: Kenny Roberts (left) and Eddy Lawson stand next to Agostini, now team manager.

Above: while visiting Maranello with Eddy Lawson, Ago plays tribute to an old acquaintance, Enzo Ferrari. Below: the complete Team Agostini, 1986.

Two motor-racing legends, two enduring stars. Jackie Stewart (left), the Formula 1 ace, and Giacomo Agostini, the motorcyclist who has won more races than any other.

Tape n° 6
Life is a game

Every now and then Agostini would call him, announcing yet another trip: Spain, Sardinia, Britain, France, Switzerland. Once he was heading off for India. To Nao, who spent nearly all his time shut away in his office, it seemed a marvellous life, one that he would probably never experience.

A comparison between one of the photos of Agostini chosen for the book and a photo of Nao's visage, when he felt good (i.e. all the time), revealed a certain resemblance: they were both wily, but with a soft demeanour that captivated, put you at ease: maybe that was why people always seemed to get *him* to do what *they* wanted.

Of course, Nao was short, fat and ugly, while Ago had the Hollywood-style good looks of the textbook Mediterranean male.

Both smiled a lot. Nao, in fact, smiled all the time, often for no reason at all.

Like Agostini, Nao could be cold and controlled: life wasn't a chess game to him the way it had been for Agostini, but it was certainly a game, one that required intelligent action, shrewdness and a will to win.

Before starting the tape he recalled the freshly trimmed lawn around the Winner's house, the superbly-kept garden, the dirt-free rim of the swimming pool, the well-ordered garage: nothing was out of place.

Order: for a professional motorcyclist it was essential. Only if everything was in order, in exactly the right place, could the racer free his mind and ride like the wind.

For instance, Agostini had driven Nao half-mad when they'd selected the photos to be published in the book. He had hundreds of them, covering every period of his life. First they'd looked at them all, then they'd looked at them all again to find the most interesting ones. At that point, as they were trying to pick the best, Agostini had attributed each photo a number and listed all the numbers on a sheet of paper; alongside each number he'd indicated the envelope or album from which the photo has been removed. At that moment Nao felt suffocated. On the one hand he felt trapped, as if his decisional scope had been reduced to zero; on the other he felt crushed by so much precision, so much thoroughness – and he was pretty damn meticulous himself (which was why, together with the fact that he asked interesting questions, Agostini had chosen him).

He recalled something that had happened just when they were browsing through the photos: the gardener-cum-dogsbody (who doubled up as waiter and driver and in this last role had the unsettling habit of jumping red lights as Nao had discovered when the miniscule Asian had picked him up at the station; he had not said anything to Agostini, who was almost certainly unaware of it) was cleaning nearby: as he wiped the ping pong table clean a ball had dropped onto the floor. Agostini had lifted his gaze off the photos and turned his head, waiting. A few seconds went by and, seeing that the gardener hadn't picked it up, he'd called, not loudly, "Jordi…". After a pause of a few seconds he repeated the man's name, a little louder. The gardener poked his head around the corner and looked at Agostini who, his voice calm and soft, said "The ball…".

Nao had smiled, and so had Agostini's secretary, who was helping out with the photos.

She was nice, just a little timid and introverted. Nao liked her.

She, unlike Agostini and himself, was a graduate and super-qualified. "Always over-qualified", she'd said, poor girl; she worked as Agostini's secretary and at a doctors' studio in the afternoons.

Yes, he liked her. To the extent that he had even considered asking her out. But she lived in another town, and seeing her would be tricky. Nevertheless, he still enjoyed the thought of her when he woke in the morning.

The decision not to ask her out had not been too hard perhaps because her attraction was more cerebral than visceral. And he had great faith in himself and his future: he still had it all ahead of him; he wasn't like Agostini, who, more than a future, had a great past in front of him.

Nevertheless the secretary was of key importance to the outcome of the book, because Agostini had told him that, as soon as the draft was ready, she would be the first to read it. Nao was pretty sure, in fact, that Ago would never actually read it himself as long as she told him it was good. He didn't know why, but Nao was convinced that was how things would go if, in her opinion, the book was a good read.

NAO When did you win your first Grand Prix?

GIACOMO At my first world championship race with MV, at the Nürburgring. It was 1965. I was up against all the champions of the moment, the greatest being Mike Hailwood. I'd got there in the evening with my Porsche and checked into a small hotel. It was half-past eight. At the doorway to the dining hall I noticed a table of Japanese people, packed with Honda's riders, mechanics and engineers. I went in, feeling as timid as a mouse. When they saw me they exchanged a few words with each other and burst out laughing. I thought they were making fun of me so I got all offended and walked back out. Perhaps they hadn't even been talking about me, but I'd won a race in Italy the week before and didn't fancy being taken for a novice. I went back to my room, and stayed there. The next day we started practice. I was entered for both the 350 and the 500. The 350 had the new three-cylinder engine, the 500 still had the old four-cylinder, which, unfortunately, was really heavy and since I wasn't particularly well-built I found it tricky to ride: I did all right, but I just didn't feel entirely comfortable on it. With that bike beating Hailwood was a tough proposition... The 350, instead, felt like it had been made for me. I'd test-ridden it, felt great on it. There was Redman with the Honda, Phil Read with the Yamaha, Bill Ivy... a hard core of competitors. We were doing the short circuit, which dropped down from the hill: it might have been only seven or so kilometres as opposed to the nearly twenty-three of the complete circuit, but it was extremely demanding. I did all right in the practice: I was always first or second, up there with the best. Unfortunately, on the Saturday the engine on the 350 broke down because of the shaft that pumps the oil through. We had no spare parts. But since your average Italian mechanic is an ingenious one we managed to rig up another shaft: it worked, but we were terrified because it was impossible to test the strength or hardness of the material. At eight in the evening I noticed the mechanics still hadn't returned to the hotel. They were still working on the engine, which was lying there in pieces, so I went back to the hotel to get some food for them. I was given soup that looked like pig swill; I took it down to them in a sort of bucket, this German soup, which really did look like something you'd feed to the pigs. Yet they were so hungry and cold they just wolfed it down with some bread, which just goes to show the incredible sacrifices they made. Anyway, they finished the bike and the next day I had the most amazing duel with Jim Redman: the two of us were out in front; at a certain point it started to drizzle and I managed to take the lead. When I glanced back he'd disappeared from view: he'd skidded off the track. That was my first World Championship win.

NAO Both your first and last world championship wins were at the Nürburgring with the MV but in 1976 you rode the 500 on the long circuit…

GIACOMO Yes, I won that first race immediately after arriving at MV, so emotions were running high and there were tears, joy… I was extremely proud to have won a world championship race on an MV, with an all-new three-cylinder 350, and delighted at having lived up to the expectations of Count Agusta. Later, in the evening I went back to the hotel and found that same group of Japanese people there, in the dining hall. I walked in quietly and they turned to look at me. Their demeanour had changed entirely: they stood up and congratulated me, making me feel really important – it was sweet revenge for the way they'd behaved the evening before.

NAO And that's where you're winning career in Grand prix motorcycling began.

GIACOMO Yes. Even though I'd already competed in a Gran Premio d'Italia at Monza with the Morini 250 and had raced in another World Championship event, again with the Morini, at the Solitude, I hadn't yet won.

NAO At the time a lot of racing was done in Germany. They had two Grand Prixs: one in the East and one in the West.

GIACOMO Yes. I remember the Sachsenring, the circuit where the East German Grand Prix was ridden. A fabulous event, attracting some 150-200 thousand people, it was a highway route and the pits were in the dusty forecourt of a nearby factory. It was dangerous too, an unending switchback that was an adventure from start to finish. You needed an invitation and special permits to travel to East Germany and even if you had them it'd still take hours to get through customs. By seven in the evening the city was dead; no-one was around. Even the traffic lights were switched off, and even the best hotel was mediocre. The people were nice enough but not overly helpful either. I remember the people returning home after work, at about five in the evening, they'd stop and buy sweets and other cheap things to take home to their children. It was all very saddening, to see these people so downtrodden, these people who had such a passion for our sport. There was this kid who I'd befriended because he used to follow me everywhere: since we were sponsored by Marlboro, I'd wanted to give him a packet of cigarettes. At first he didn't want them; later on he took them - and hid them: if they were found, he explained, he'd be put in prison. Imagine it, living like that... Anyway, after the qualifying sessions it looked like we were on for one hell of a race and the public were lapping it up. After the race, though, you would see this ocean of people moving off quietly, all their zeal spent - almost joylessly I would say - to the coaches. They were good people, but it all seemed so gloomy. Once, Dieter Braun, from West Germany, won; when he went up on the podium, the public jumped to their feet, started cheering and began to get quite restless. Suddenly, from under the grandstand, some 500 policemen appeared; no-one had even suspected their presence. They pointed their machine guns directly into the crowd of fifty thousand. It was chilling. The crowd shut up instantly: the creepiest thing was that the police had foreseen and prepared for the whole thing without anyone even realising it. Another time, towards the end of qualifying, Hailwood and I were fighting it out for pole position. We were the only two left on the track and the organisers let us ride an extra half-hour because they thought the two of us were putting on quite a show. We kept breaking the track record, me on one lap with the MV, Hailwood on the next with his Honda. Yet it was a circuit that carried some seriousness sadness with it too because it was where Bill Ivy[(1)], a fantastic chap, had died. He'd been riding a Jawa 350 and I remember we'd set off on qualifying runs; a short while afterwards we were stopped because of oil on the track. Some took off their helmets while others just unclipped the chinstrap and kept it on loosely to ward off the light rain. Ivy was one of the latter. When they cleaned the track and the race director gave us the all-clear, everyone hurriedly jumped back on their bikes and roared off. I put my helmet back on. Ivy forgot to do up his chin strap, push-started the bike and rode off. He came into a bend, the engine seized, he fell and his helmet flew off. To complete his misfortune, he struck a pillar that was in the middle of an otherwise open lawn: that was how

NOTE:[(1)] Bill Ivy (GB 1942) won the 125 cc World Championship in '67 and 21 Grand Prixs in 125 and 250. He died in '69 at the Sachsenring during the East German GP.

he died. Like I've said before, the circuits of yesteryear could be fantastic, but there were no safeguards… In 1967, again at the Sachsenring, I was leading the 500 cc race when, on the last lap but one, I fell because of an oil patch: I initially managed to stay on the tarmac, then ended up in a ditch that separated the track from the field. I was doing 240 kph and was catapulted away from the motorbike. The impact broke my nose; fortunately the skin, not the bone, was peeled back completely. They took me to the pits, then held a sort of mask, onto which a rudimentary anaesthetic had been sprayed, against my face and started stitching up my nose. I remember saying "Make it look good, for the girls". They then transferred me to the hospital where they wanted to keep me in for at least a night: it was bleak beyond belief, a sort of warehouse packed with some 300 people, many of whom were groaning in distress. It made me, I admit it now, cry. I just couldn't help it. I gathered up my things and slinked away, back to the hotel. An hour later the police came to take me back to the hospital. They kept me in for observation that one night and then released me.

NAO What was the rider's life like? What happened after the races?

GIACOMO In Germany the organisers would throw a really good party the evening after the race: dancing and plenty of food… Since there were no great shows or events going on in that part of the world the party would attract the most beautiful girls in town. And I mean beautiful. We generally just enjoyed a relaxing evening, which made us forget about everything else we'd been through. Just as beautiful were the prizes: they'd give you Bohemian crystal, made in Czechoslovakia. The people were great: they'd wait for you in the hotel foyer in the morning for an autograph or just to catch a glimpse of you. They'd crowd around the car to admire it

NAO Well, it was the Eastern bloc.

GIACOMO Czechoslovakia was also full of beautiful women. Riders would be only too willing to go there and there were plenty who had girlfriends and fiancés. I was well known and well-liked there: being the absolute winner has its own sort of charm. Those who came second had less charm. I also had Italian friends who lived there. Girls would chase me all the time. I remember this stupendous twenty-four-year-old who I invited to dinner. Unknown to me, her *husband* had accompanied her to the hotel, and then we had a meal together. Her husband waited in a bar and came back later to pick her up. When she told me all this I told her that in Italy it would be unthinkable: she simply said that she'd told her husband she liked me and wanted to spend some time with me. Different strokes for different folks.

NAO And what happened after dinner?

GIACOMO Mmmhh... Probably best not to write about that. Anyway, the same thing happened to me in France: I won a race, a model presented me with the trophy and I invited her to dinner and then on to the hotel; at a certain point the phone rang and it was her boyfriend or husband telling me that he was waiting and could I ask her whether she was going to be much longer! Like the Czech girl she'd simply told her partner that she wanted to be with me, whether he liked it or not. To say that the foreigners were more open-minded than us would be an understatement. One night I was with Jim Redman at Spa-Francorchamps; even though he had just purchased a Ferrari and had the most wonderful wife, he was sleeping in a caravan. They dined with me at my hotel. Afterwards I went out for a stroll and when I came back they were on their way out. As it was Saturday night they invited me for a drink. We both had races the next day, both in the 500. "No thanks", I said, "we've got the race tomorrow". "Come on", he replied, "it's good to get out, it's good to make love too". "Maybe for you", I said, "but not for me". The next day I won. Another time, at Cesenatico, I was participating in both the 350 and then the 500. Prior to the 500 there was the 250. During the wait I climbed aboard the MV lorry to lie back on my chair. A short while later a mechanic told me a girl wanted to say hello to me: I still had the second race to come and said, no, I'd rather rest. Yet I couldn't help asking "What's she like?" "Very pretty", he replied. So I got out of the chair and looked through the peephole and saw this stunning girl. I told the mechanic to let her in: I was twenty-seven and she must have been twenty-two. She seemed glad to meet me but when I came closer to give her a kiss she drew back. So I invited her to dinner – and she turned me down. I just didn't get it: she wanted to meet me but wouldn't accept my invitation? Soon after she said she had to go but she was glad she had met me. As she left I looked through the peephole again and saw her together with a young man and a baby who couldn't have been more than two months old. She really had just wanted to meet me. I'm convinced its all just a question of mindset: a girl from another country might have left the husband with the baby and accepted the invitation.

NAO How would you describe the relationship between two people who get together purely for physical reasons?

GIACOMO Well, boys will be boys, especially where there's a good-looking girl. And women are instinctively drawn to the star, the champion: they put you on a pedestal so it's very hard not to take advantage of that in the form of a one-night stand. When a girl, who has seen you on TV as this unattainable man she dreams of holding in her arms, meets you in the flesh then I think she sees it as a one-off opportunity. Love doesn't come into it.

NAO So she gives herself willingly. But how do you see it?

GIACOMO It's a physical thing. But because you can chose from among the most attractive, you feel gratified too. It's like going to a restaurant and really enjoying a dish that you like: if you go to Modena and eat a well-cooked plate of *tortellini*, you don't just eat it, you *taste* it. It's not just sex, it's sex with *flavour*.

NAO So there was no involvement on your part?

GIACOMO No: we liked each other, there was give and take, sometimes it was great, sometimes it wasn't so great.

NAO Who used who?

GIACOMO I think we used each other. But I say it again, it's the kind of woman that makes the difference: a woman with a touch of class is different from one you might find, say, walking along the street. There are women who want to meet you and get to know you because they've seen you in the papers, on television and have probably dreamt about you: it's almost as if they'd already met you.

NAO But doesn't that just make the champion a bit of a sex object for women?

GIACOMO Well, I wouldn't go that far. There are different situations: there are those that just want to meet you and those that say "I want to marry you". Everyone has their own reasons.

NAO What did you talk about with them?

GIACOMO They talked about their lives. Over dinner we'd chat about the usual things: they'd ask about my sport or try to find out some new detail about my life, or I'd tell them how a race had gone, pretty much the same stuff every time. Like I said, because I was in the public eye, in a sense they already knew me, so it was all so much easier: they'd talk to me the way you'd talk to an acquaintance. I often meet people who immediately call me by my first name: they do so because they've known me forever, perhaps have photos of me, have read about me. I'm not a stranger to them. When I was touring Australia I was the guest of a rich Australian who had his wife accompany me around. This twenty-seven year old woman, perhaps because I was so famous over there, gave herself to me utterly. We were together all day for eight or nine days and it almost blossomed into something a bit more serious. It was beautiful. I say it again: the women outside Italy were very different. And so were the men: I'd never tell *my* wife to escort a man around all day.

Nao stopped the tape.

He recalled how, at that point in the interview, he'd drunk a cup of coffee: the memory of this made him feel like one now, so he went into the kitchen to make it. While he was doing so he thought about what had then happened at Agostini's house.

That day his wife hadn't been there. Maria was blond, beautiful with graceful lines – and very kind. It was always her who offered Nao coffee, and when she brought it to him he felt content.

During the interview he'd begun to feel a touch tired, so he asked if he could have a coffee. Since no-one else was in the house Agostini declared they would have to make it themselves. As he didn't drink coffee himself, he wasn't used to making it - but he'd do his best.

Nao was struck by the slowness and precision with which Agostini tipped spoonfuls of coffee powder into the filter of the moka: each time he added a spoonful he pressed the powder down gently. When the coffee finally came, Nao was surprised to see that the teaspoon belonged to KLM airlines. He'd smiled, but without explaining why to Agostini, who'd asked him. It was simple really: at home, Nao's only teaspoons were the ones he'd collected from the various airlines he'd flown with.

He restarted the tape.

GIACOMO In South Africa, during a two or three-race tour, I was Mike Hailwood's guest in South Africa. Like Jim Redman, he'd gone to live in Durban and had set himself up in this terrific villa complete with swimming pool. They'd organise parties where we'd have one hell of a time; they'd always invite plenty of women and, as we were young and famous the outcome was often inevitable. One particular aspect comes to mind: we'd go along to the parties at seven and by half past eleven it would all be over. If only it were like that in Italy! Here the parties start at one in the morning and finish at five in the morning, so the next day you're knackered. Not only that, between half-nine and one you're often at a loose end… All because it's "in" to get to the disco late. To my mind it's not healthy at all. I just don't understand why we can't enjoy ourselves for the same number of hours but just get there and leave at more reasonable times. That sort of schedule never went down very well with me because I've never liked staying up to the small hours. If you enjoy yourself earlier and get it out of you're system then you're more rested the next day. Anyway, in South Africa we were – motorcycling and training apart – interested in the girls and the parties. At Hailwood's villa you'd leave the car in the garage and walk straight into the bedroom. Oh, and they used to drink a lot more than I did.

NAO Did you not drink much?

GIACOMO I wasn't too keen on it. Every now and again I'd have a whisky and ginger: it tasted alcoholic but it was ginger with a dash of whisky more than anything else. I don't think you need to drink to enjoy yourself. Of course, when you've had a few you let yourself go, you're happier: but I didn't need it - I was happy and in high spirits without it anyway.

NAO How were you paid on those occasions?

GIACOMO The organisers paid us an allowance and all our expenses, but only after the race. In places where you were already trusted they'd give you half before the race and half after, otherwise you'd usually get everything at the end. Accommodation, food and the car were paid for. In Australia, for instance, where I stayed ten days I was picked up at the airport in a Rolls-Royce with darkened windows, a car I'd only ever seen on television. It was embarrassing, I was treated like royalty. Not that I expected it, though, but the Australians have always treated me with a certain regard. I've had some great moments, sometimes getting the full superstar treatment. No problems of any kind, everything organised – I didn't have to think about a thing.

NAO Being treated like that at the age of twenty-five must have felt good.

GIACOMO Yeah, it's all a bit of a dream. But I've always kept my feet on the ground; whether I went out for dinner with the President of Italy or factory workers it made no difference. Sure, whenever I went to Emilia Romagna I could easily have gone without any ID or my wallet as I would have had no use for them. Even now, even though I haven't raced for thirty years, the same thing still happens to me. Last week I went to Rimini and Forlì: there were three hotels I could have stayed at and I had four invitations to dinner. People still remember me even now, so imagine what it was like when I was

World Champion and was winning every Sunday: all the doors would be opened, there was always a place for me. It's incredibly gratifying but you have to be careful not to make the mistake of taking it all for granted. Some say they do it to thank you for the joy you've given them, as fans: that's really nice, I like that. At Forlì, a well-to-do man said he wanted to thank me for all the thrills I'd given him when he was young. There's never any problem, especially in Emilia-Romagna, in finding an invitation to dinner. Of course it happens because you're a celebrity but you must never think its owed you, otherwise it can all backfire. You can't just take advantage of it – you have to give something back in return. Sometimes fame drives people crazy because, when it's all over, they just can't readjust to reality. You have to watch it.

NAO Tell me about the *Temporada romagnola*.

GIACOMO It was the race you waited all winter for because it marked the start of the season. Emilia Romagna had the liveliest crowds of all: Modena, Imola, Cesenatico, Riccione and Milano Marittima brought us back to life after our winter hibernation. So the Temporada was both a competition and a crucial training session. It was exciting to leave a sedate place like Bergamo and go to the Romagna, the hearty home of motor sports. The event was a question mark - you wondered who would be invited. Will Jim Redman be there with Honda? And Tom Phillis on the other Honda? What about Taveri on the five-cylinder Honda? Maybe they've signed up Phil Read and Pasolini is sure to be there… The fans would go wild. At Modena, where the first event was held in mid-March, they once had to close the gates at eleven in the morning because the facility was packed to the point of being dangerous. There, you raced right next to the crowd, almost skimming the people. One fan wanted me to skim by close enough to put his cigarette out. Track invasions and post-race parties were the order of the day and afterwards we'd all go and eat splendidly. There was that girl who came to see me in the truck too. At Riccione Hailwood and I met two sisters from Imola who became our girlfriends: while they split up after just two or three months we stayed together for about a year. At Cesenatico - or it might have been Rimini or Milano Marittima – there was a fisherman who, once he'd landed his catch, would invite us to his place and barbecue the fresh fish… It was exquisite: I've not eaten such tasty fish since. Racing was a job, but we all had such a good time – especially the non-Italian riders – that we looked forward to the event enormously, even if there wasn't much money involved.

NAO As the star you earned more though, didn't you?

GIACOMO There were few prizes. Some got more favourable contracts based on the previous year's performance or how big their names were getting. I think the going rate back then was 300,000 liras per race. Of course, the champion always got preferential treatment.

NAO You were challenged many times at the *Temporada* and were sometimes beaten by track-specific specialists, yet on the longer circuits you'd take your revenge. Take Pasolini for instance...

GIACOMO I won more than I lost at the *Temporada* but every now and then I'd get whipped. When Pasolini was in front of a home crowd he could put in 120 percent. It would work out quite well in a way because at the next race there'd be twice as many people. But outside Italy, where I suffered the absence of supporters less than he did, things generally went my way.

NAO Was the *Temporada romagnola* an important event?

GIACOMO Sure it was. It was valid for the Italian Championship. The support from the fans was incredible. I once beat Pasolini at Riccione and the crowd was livid because I'd overtaken him on the last bend. I had to hide in the ambulance and they took me away as if I'd been injured; emotions were running so high there was a fear I might be attacked. At Pesaro, when Saarinen was given a Benelli, I was beaten because one of my exhaust pipes dropped off: it had been a close fight that in the end was taken by Saarinen. All hell broke loose! Everyone immediately forgot that the exhaust had come off and started saying "Agostini has been beaten by Saarinen on the Benelli!". You would have thought it was the end of the world! I think I behaved fairly though, because I didn't give much importance to the fact that Saarinen had won because of the broken exhaust. Later, though, my pride got the better of me and I came out with it because I *knew* it hadn't been my fault – but it looked like an excuse and no-one believed me, not even when I showed them the exhaust. If it had been less of a close-run thing I still might have won, but in races like that... Everyone had their own clan. Even Jim Redman had his henchman. So did Mike Hailwood: his 'minder' was a hotel owner who would put him up and take good care of him. As you might imagine, all these different groups had it in for me: the atmosphere could get quite electric at times. Yet my memories of all this are wonderful because apart from the victories there was this breathtaking atmosphere: the public, the knife-edge races... One of the last times I raced at Riccione the roads were lined with sixty thousand fans. Where can you get sixty thousand fans nowadays? At Imola there'd be 100-120 thousand. To get them in the gates would be opened at five in the morning. You'd be virtually swathed in fans, in a very affectionate, not oppressive way. Coming out of the hotel I felt like the President of the Republic: no matter how early it was there'd always be someone waiting for me. One evening I got back at eleven and they told me an entire family, children included, had been waiting there for four hours me. We said hello, shook hands and then off they went. They were what I call real fans.

NAO What did they call you back then?

GIACOMO My best friend called me Mino, a diminutive of Giacomino. In Great Britain they called me Ago, in France Ago le roi, the king. These days the nickname that sticks is Ago, but most people simply call me by my Christian name, Giacomo, because that's how my wife has always referred to me. Nevertheless, for old friends I'm still Mino, and for the fans I'm still Ago.

Nao didn't call him Mino or Ago, just Giacomo. Perhaps it was just a way of maintaining the right balance, the proper distance.

Yet when he thought about the book, Nao thought of him as the Winner, not Giacomo or Giacomo Agostini. Yes, he'd re-baptised him. It was his way of making him his, having him closer – and being able to write about him.

Without knowing why, money came to mind.

Nao enjoyed checking his cashpoint receipts and seeing how much was left in his account, watching his capital accrue little by little. Perhaps the Winner did the same – albeit with rather different figures, mused Nao.

Tape n° 7
Being aware that everything comes to an end

The waiter tripped, only just managing to retain his balance.

"Dinner *and* a show" Nao quipped to the girl at the next table. They both smiled. A well-timed stroke of luck like that, which paves the way for further conversation, is a rarity, mused Nao.

"That's life: some times you trip and don't fall, some times you trip *and* fall", he continued.

"How profound", she wisecracked.

Nao chuckled.

"Nice to meet you, Carlo".

"Sara".

"*Very* nice to meet you, Sara".

"Whoa, handing out the complements already?".

"Okay, what do you do?".

"I'm in sales, electrical appliances. You?".

"Journalist".

"Great profession".

"Yep. Plenty of travelling, you know how it is. And every day's different, always something new to see and learn. Yes, it's good".

She looked around, observing the ambiance of the restaurant.

"Nice place. Do you come here often?", asked Nao.

"Sometimes".

"Always alone?".

"No. I'm waiting for a couple of girlfriends. They're late".

"I like the music they put on here".

She didn't answer. Nao looked at her more carefully. She was blond, her hair cut short. Her gently-outlined face gave her a kind air. The bluish hue under her eyes were, thought Nao, attractive. She certainly wasn't like most of the women Nao encountered during his nocturnal outings.

It was, in truth, Nao's first time in this restaurant. It could be said that it was a little more elegant – no, a little less squalid – than the places he usually ate at.

As she'd arrived before her he hadn't seen her sit at the table: he wandered what her lower half looked like. She had nice breasts, not too big, yet her hips and bottom, which were of greater interest to him, remained hidden below the table.

"Have you got a boyfriend?", he asked her.

"No. But I've already met the man of my life. I'm just waiting for him to come and whisk me away".

"How do you mean?".

"You know when you meet someone and just know they're the *one*? Well, that's what happened to me".

"So how come he hasn't whisked you away yet?".

"Because he's French, lives a long way away and is terribly busy. He's a mountain climber and right now he's only got time for mountains and climbing them. I don't get it really. When he texts me he always speaks about the coming climb and how difficult it's going to be. Well, I do understand him, I suppose: he just has to follow his instinct, do what he wants".

"And how about you. What's your plan? To wait around?".

"Of course. One day he'll realise I'm here and come and get me".

"Why don't you go to him?"

"Hmm. I don't know. I might just do that".

"If he really is the one, you should, shouldn't you?".

"Oh, he's definitely the one for me. I know he is".

"And why's that?".

"First, he's gorgeous. Second, we share a lot of interests and we can talk for hours and hours. In short, I like him – lots".

"When did you meet?".

"About eight months ago".

"Where?".

"In Germany, for a trade fair. We're both in sales. See? Another thing in common".

"How many times have you seen him?".

"Just the once".

"And that was enough for you to decide he's the only man for you?".

"Yes. We met in the jacuzzi of the hotel we were staying at. I was already in and then he arrived and asked if I minded him getting in with me, which I thought was very polite of him. I said yes of course: I'd already decided I liked him. Although it's not the thing that interests me the most he does have a stunning body; he's an ex bodybuilder and now climbs mountains. Anyway, we talked for quite a bit and he never once took his eyes off mine. We stayed in there until I felt stewed - the water was really hot. After, he invited out me out to dinner. It was a romantic meal and we did a lot more talking".

"And then?".

"We went back to the hotel and he said: 'How does the evening end?'".

"And you said?".

"Asleep, in our own rooms".

"Oh, come on. The man of your life and you send him off to sleep in another room?".

"Yes. He was sorry about that, and he told me so. But it had to be so".

"Why?".

"For the precise reason that I liked him so much, had such a strong feeling about him. It seemed special. If I'd liked him less I'd have taken him to bed with me. After all, why not? A great-looking guy, it would have been nice. But I already knew there was a lot more to it".

"And you haven't seen each other since?".

"No".

"But you talk, right?"

"He just texts me, once a week on average, and I do the same".

"When he texts, do you reply?".

"Not necessarily. I've tried not texting, to see the effect. He texted me".

Nao looked at her: she was really pretty, naïve and pure. Yes, she was nothing like the girls he usually met. She was so far from his world that, truth be told, he wouldn't have known what to do with such a girl.

Given her story, he didn't even bother asking for her phone number. There was little left to do except finish up, get up and move on.

He said goodbye. She replied politely, and looked into his eyes for a fraction of a second, just long enough not to appear rude. She was one of those nice girls whose always a little afraid of offending. Sensitive, he would say.

As he left, Nao realised she had never really spoken with him at all; she had spoken with the love of her life; telling the story to a complete stranger was her way of rekindling the flame, the insane dream that burned inside her, and doing so had probably made her happy.

He went back home. It was late but he was feeling wound up. Tiredness eluded him.

The nice girl at the restaurant came to mind. He wished she'd *really* spoken to him.

Why is it, he wondered, that women just do not seem to understand it when a man just wants to make love, to be nice, to receive some tender loving care? Why do they never get it? Why so many questions, so many problems? Why do they spend so much time dreaming and then, for the most part, settle for the exact opposite of what they dreamt of?

All said and done, Nao thought, it was only harmless no-strings sex, was it not? Something pleasant, fleeting, without the fallout of heartache, phone calls or text messages or anguished questions like "If I call now what will he think?". Why is it that a red-blooded male who simply wants to do what nature intended is left only with the whores and the dogs?

He settled down to work. Work, he pondered, is the only thing that never lets you down. When you're alone and want to stop the thoughts flowing, when you don't feel like going out, work will see you through. And you get paid too! Getting paid for feeling better, contemplated Nao, is something quite extraordinary.

He'd reached the end of the last tape. All that was left were the notes he'd jotted down hurriedly in the car one day after he realised the recorder had failed to pick up the interview properly: the batteries had been nearly flat, strong enough to turn the tape but not record the conversation. It happens.

Nao had taken it as a sign: something had changed, perhaps it was time to stop interviewing, perhaps the research had been done.

In any case, every story has to have an ending.

Moreover, he had run out of questions to ask. His curiosity was exhausted, his thirst for information quenched. During that last interview he had, for the first time since he'd started seeing Agostini, felt the pangs of boredom. Given this, Nao had decided his work was at an end. Just as the Winner had taken those strange accidents as a sign that his career was over, so Nao saw the unrecorded tape as a sign.

He pressed the 'play' button to listen to Agostini's words, which gradually began to fade away as the recorder's batteries faltered, and then consulted the notes he'd scribbled in the car.

Disjointed words and phrases reached his ears. No questions from Nao could be heard: there were just a few random memories that had popped into Agostini's mind as they'd scanned the photo albums.

GIACOMO Motorcycling has been the love of my life. I've dreamt about it since I was born. Motorcycling has given me so much – everything, really. It has given me thrills that would otherwise have been unimaginable. I find it bizarre when, for instance, I hear of a rider who was previously a football player: for me it's always been motorcycles and nothing else. See this photo? It's the MV racing department. Whenever I was tired, had a headache or just felt down I'd take off to Cascina Costa, and when I got there I'd feel better immediately: the problem would evaporate. Then I'd return home happy. I'd be whistling, pleased because I'd seen my motorcycles, my engines. Perhaps my mechanics – those terrific mechanics - would tell me they were preparing some special cylinders: even though the cylinders might, in truth, have been useless, the simple fact that that they were working for me made me feel great. One winter, for example, a mechanic was assigned to me and me alone, his task being to lighten the engine. We were racing against Yamaha and their two-stroke engine weighed a whopping twenty kilos less than ours. He worked all winter to get the weight down and every time I saw him hard at work it really gave me a buzz, as if he'd somehow injected a few extra horsepower.

The Winner would always present Nao to his friends as "my biographer". Nao loved this accolade, it made him puff his chest out. When a colleague had called him to say that Agostini was referring to him thus, Nao had jumped up and down all around the room, his face warped by the daft smile he always had whenever he was happy: "His biographer! ... His biographer! ..." he'd yelped. Oh yes, he loved the idea of being someone's biographer, the one who knows more than anybody else about a famous person, enough to write a book, a biography, a life story. At the end of the day, though, it wasn't as if Nao knew that much about him. He still hadn't analysed all those facts and dates and he wasn't sure he wanted to. He honestly didn't feel like picking holes in the Winner's life and it seemed as if he already knew everything about him as it was.

"Who knows what's next?", he asked, delighted at the unpredictable turn his life seemed (to him, anyway) to be taking.

His thoughts stopped their wandering and Nao got back to work. Presented with a photo of Agostini surrounded by the usual clutch of beauties. Nao has asked "But didn't it bother you, giving up all those occasional girlfriends?".

GIACOMO No, because the motorbike was my true love. You have to understand that I had friends, male and female, at the Tourist Trophy, then I'd leave for Holland where I had another group of friends who'd make me forget about the TT ones and afterwards I'd move on to Belgium where other friends and acquaintances would make me forget the ones in Holland. I never had the time to stop and think or feel sad about what I'd left behind. It was all so fast that I never had time to develop a bond, We'd see each other for four or five days, then I'd be gone and we might not even see each other until the next year. One day I was at the airport, about to go to Australia and as I was checking in this very pretty girl standing behind me said, "I know you're going to Australia... So am I. Can you tell me your seat number so I can sit with you on the way?". She'd learnt I was going to Australia from the newspapers, so she'd bought herself a ticket. She'd planned everything. In the end she stayed with me for the whole month. She was wonderful. Only after we got to know each other a bit did she confess she'd made the trip just to be with me. It was wonderful: a young, bright girl – who'd only recently got married... She was a few years older than me: I was twenty six and she must have been twenty-eight or thirty. She had money too: she took me to all the very best hotels and restaurants. What a journey it was... Of course, she did stop me meeting a lot of other women I might otherwise have encountered over there...

Nao wasn't envious of the Winner. He could have been, given the envious life he'd had. Of course he would have loved to have been Agostini, with all that money and all those women – but so what. In fact, he felt as if he were quite similar to Agostini. He felt on a par with him, right at the same level. The fact that this feeling, as anyone would have been able to confirm, was totally unfounded, didn't worry him the least because he would never tell anyone what he thought anyway. He would never ask anyone what they thought he should or shouldn't do and the reason was simple: he *knew* what he had to do. Because, yes, Nao knew the way of the world. Oh, yes, he certainly knew that. He knew where he was going, didn't lose control and would never be swallowed up by the loafers who are always trying to sell you something, always trying to get something from you. He knew what was going on, what he was doing and which road to take – and maybe it was the latter that was the most important of all.

At that point the tape petered out, leaving only the hiss of static. Nao picked up his notepad, which he'd saved for last.

He read that Agostini had told him he'd discovered, after long and hard thought, a way of increasing the number of garages in a block of flats he was completing (his career, these days, was the construction of luxury homes in Bergamo). Into a space that seemed made for no more than twenty-seven garages he had managed to fit thirty.

Then he'd gone on to say that not having been nominated Motor Sportsman of the Century had really bugged him when the award was given at the end of the nineties. It had been won by racing car driver Alain Prost. "How do you judge champions from different eras and disciplines? By the titles, the number of titles he's won, which is the only way not to make a biased choice. So why did Prost win and not me? He won four racing car titles, I won *fifteen* in motorcycling. So how is that?". The Winner was in no doubt he was the best and wanted others to acknowledge it too. And he hated it when it didn't happen, especially when it was for political reasons.

Nao raised his head from the notes. He started pacing about the room. For no special reason the Winner's hands came to mind: they were small, almost child-like – but strong. It occurred to him that the real champion shows himself only when in difficulty: his greatness lies not in never falling, but in his ability to get up and carry on when he does.

He started reading again.

That same day, Agostini had also told him about the duels with the cocky young locals on the Riviera of Lake Iseo: riding his Guzzi Lodola 175 (certainly no racing machine) he had thrashed them all.

A friend of his – also his first manager – placed the bets and withdrew the winnings.

He'd also gone on to say that he should really have won seventeen world titles, not fifteen: one was lost when he broke his shoulder in the accident with Barry Sheene and another in the last race of the season with the 350 in Japan.

In the accident with Barry Sheene, in Sweden in '74, Agostini had been slipstreaming Sheene and had decided to postpone his overtaking manoeuvre to the fast bend further on, his plan being to take the curve tight and pass him on the inside. He'd already drawn level with him two bends before but had decided to wait. At the next bend, though, with Agostini just inches behind him, Sheene had fallen because of water leaking from his radiator and Agostini had inevitably ploughed into him: he fell with Sheene and broke his shoulder. "Bastard!" he hollered, as he lay there (not that it was Sheene's fault at all, it was due to a mechanical problem, but there was no way Agostini could have known that). His shoulder was operated on by the same surgeon who'd just operated on Thoeni: the surgeon had begun to make a name for himself with these operations. In fact, he was the only one to gain anything from all this, finding fame in Italy through their misfortune. Among other things, he'd put Teflon in Agostini's shoulder (this might not even have been necessary) and so the Winner off was the bike for a month, missing three races and losing out on another world title.

Then, when they came to photos of his children, Agostini, who had hoped to see his son follow a motorcycling career, had said that Giacomino had, it seemed, developed a passion for soccer: it was his daughter, Vittoria, who was interested in the bikes. But being a girl he had decided not to encourage her.

The words of the Winner had ended. Now it was time to get down to some serious writing.

Nao stopped. For the first time he thought deeply about what he should say about Giacomo Agostini, what type of book he should write.

"Will it ever get published if I decide to write it the way it should be written?", wondered Nao. And then, but only for an instant, he asked himself: "Why did they ask me to write the Winner's story?".

He would have liked to write about Agostini the way he'd seen him during the interviews - his obsessions and trifles, his vices and virtues, his nit-picking precision - and not just praise and glorify him for the champion he had been and the celebrity he still was.

All said and done, though, what did he care anyway? When he handed over the draft he'd get, independently of how it was written, an advance payment and that was the money he needed most urgently; yes, that should see him right. They could change the title, mutilate the prose and put his name next to Agostini's or not (the latter option was preferred by the editor he felt it would boost sales – and he was probably right about that). He'd take the money and head for Cuba, a place he'd been longing to see for years. Let someone else take all the credit, he thought: dancing cheek to cheek with a gorgeous Cuban in the moonlight was, instead, of much more interest to wily old Nao. A fortnight's vacation in Cuba: that was something that would make him, in his own special way, feel like a winner.

APPENDICES

An astonishing career

If numbers mean anything at all, Giacomo Agostini is an astounding motorcycle rider. He has won more motorcycle races than anyone else in motorcycling history: fifteen World Championship titles in ten years in both the 350 and 500 cc categories (two more than Angel Nieto, six more than Mike Hailwood and Carlo Ubbiali). It is all the more breathtaking because ten titles were won consecutively, when he achieved the 350-500 double from 1968 to 1972. He won one hundred and twenty two GPs (forty-six more than his arch-enemy Hailwood, thirty-two more than his closest rival, Nieto) out of one hundred and seventy seven. That in itself is another record. He was Italian Champion eighteen times, taking his first title in 1963 and his last in 1977. Throughout his career, he won a staggering three hundred and eleven races. In short, there has never been a greater Champion.

Brescia-born but now resident in Bergamo, Giacomo Agostini, Mino to his friends and Ago for everyone else, was not only the top motorcycle rider of his day: he was also the first to become a celebrity, a true star. The generation of champions that preceded him, the last of whom was Ubbiali, were more 'motorcycle performers' than personalities. A quarter of a century would pass after Agostini's retirement before another such star would shine, Valentino Rossi, the wonder-boy from Tavullia. World famous and immensely popular, these brilliant, brave riders have become true protagonists of the star system in much the same way as Formula 1 drivers Juan Manuel Fangio, Ayrton Senna and Michael Shumacher. Through talent, bravery and success, they have all left a mark on our collective imaginations.

Agostini was the most famous rider of the 70s and even now, so many years after his retirement from competition, people still remember him fondly.

He was a champion of determination, self-denial and concentration. Little of the highlife, little luxury (his villa, with swimming-pool and sauna, above Bergamo, was practical more than it was swish) and lots of sweat. He learnt to ride a bicycle at the age of two, then moved on to the obstacle races in the villages. At 19 he took part in his first proper race and came second: but coming second would prove to be the exception, not the rule, and he soon became accustomed to the top of the podium. His outstanding skills immediately gave him the opportunity to become the official rider for Morini. Yet his longest-lasting partnership would be with MV Agusta, who offered him three and four-cylinders machines that made him unbeatable. He has enjoyed great victories against riders like Hailwood, Redman, Saarinen, Pasolini, Bergamonti, Read, Cecotto, Sheene and Lucchinelli. He never wanted any other top dogs on the team (in the end, in 1973, he was forced to ride alongside Phil Read, a very tough customer) because when it came to winning, all that was needed was Agostini. Angelo Bergamonti, a talented rider who had been taken on by MV to plug the second rider gap with little expected of him, died trying to keep pace with Agostini at Riccione on 4th April 1971.

Ago became an idol, appearing in photo-story magazines and films: with his handsome features and piercing green eyes he embodied the very idea of the champion, the winner. Yet he never took it for granted and remained utterly professional in his approach to training and relations with the team, the people and the racing game in general. He never drank and was always in peak physical condition (1.7 metres tall, weighing 66 kilos). He was near-fanatical when it came to tuning the bike and he never left anything to chance, on the track or off it. You could say he always made the right decisions, and the world of motorcycling acknowledged his intelligence and perceptiveness in this because in the end it's a world where you win because of your knowledge, not your athletic performance.

The accusation of having won so much because he had the best bikes was always levelled at him. And who could deny it ? But the point is that the best motorbikes nearly always go to the best riders, and every time there was a direct confrontation, Agostini won. At the beginning of his career, just after joining MV, he had to face Hailwood, who was in tip-top condition and already a veteran: it was tough. Yet when Hailwood, in 1966 and 1967, was racing with Honda, they fought on an equal footing, resulting in some of the most fascinating moments in motorcycling where neither the result nor the winner were the main issue (in 1967, for example, Ago had five wins, as did "Mike the Bike", but the title went to Agostini for the best overall performance.) After Hailwood's retirement, Agostini completely dominated in the 350 and the 500 cc classes throughout 1968, 1969 and 1970, winning every world championship GP he took part in.

Then, in 1971 and 1972, he came up against Jarno Saarinen and Renzo Pasolini, two dazzling riders who could count on fast motorbikes with powerful two-strokes, the Yamaha and the Aermacchi: for two years they made life hard for Agostini, who nevertheless kept on winning. In 1973 the battle stepped up a gear: there was the arrival of another antagonist - Read - at MV and the Yamaha 500 was competition-ready (with this motorbike, Saarinen would win the two first GPs of the season in the 500 class). Tragically, on May 20th, two of motorcycling's best-loved protagonists and the season's favourites, Saarinen and Pasolini, were killed on the track at Monza. At the end of that year, Ago lost the 500 cc title but won the 350 cc.

In 1974 Ago joined Yamaha and a year later, he became the 500 cc World Champion, winning for the first time with a two stroke engine on a Japanese motorcycle. It was a motorcycling milestone, as was his astonishing win at the Daytona 200 in 1974 on a Yamaha 700.

Later, when Yamaha pulled out and he found himself (in 1976) without a factory bike, he started from scratch, setting up his own team which used two self-managed MV Agusta 350 and 500 motorbikes. Overall, it was a disastrous season in which he was forced to retire in twelve races out of sixteen: nevertheless, he still managed to notch up another two Grand Prix wins.

Once he realised that his motorcycling career had run its course, Agostini tried his hand with cars. He raced for three years and while the results were respectable, time was no longer on his side. Rather than insist, he stepped sideways to become a World Motorcycling Championship team manager, a role that allowed him to exploit his unequalled experience, determination and precision to the full. And thanks to the talent of a taciturn American, Eddie Lawson, Agostini won another three titles – this time from the paddocks - in the 500 class.

A life in the fast lane

1942 Born on 16th June in Brescia to parents Maria Vittoria and Aurelio Agostini. Eldest of four sons, he was followed by Gabriele (1947), Mauro (1952) and Felice (1955). Lived in the village of Cividate Camuno (Brescia) until the age of thirteen.
1955 Family moves to Lovere on Lake Iseo
1961 First race (the Trento-Bondone hill race)
1963 Becomes official rider for Morini at start of season
1963 Makes his debut in the World Championship (250 Morini) at the Italian GP in Monza
1963 Wins his first two Italian championships (junior), on hill climbs and circuits with a Morini 175 cc
1964 Wins the first Italian Senior Championship on a Morini 250
1965 Joins MV Agusta
1965 First win in a World Championship GP at only his fourth attempt (in Germany at the Nürburgring, 350 cc category, on an MV Agusta).
1966 First World Championship title (500 cc category): no Italian had won the 500 cc World Championship title since 1957 (Libero Liberati on a Gilera).
1966 First Isle of Man TT victory.
1970 First rider to win the TT three times running (Senior on a 500, and Junior on a 350).
1971 Establishes new lap record at the Grad Prix of Nations in Monza (which as yet remains unbeaten) with an average speed of 204.545 kilometres per hour.
1971 Nominated "Official Cavalier of the Republic" by Giuseppe Saragat
1972 Last victory at the Isle of Man TT, completing a winning

streak of 10 consecutive wins.

1972 Wins his 13th Italian championship title, beating Tarquinio Provini's record of 12 titles.

1973 Builds a villa on the hills overlooking Bergamo and settles there.

1974 Leaves MV Agusta and joins Yamaha.

1974 Wins Daytona 200-mile race (on the Yamaha 700).

1975 His last - and fifteenth - World Championship title: the first 500 cc World Championship title to be won with a two-stroke engine.

1976 On 29th August wins his last GP in the 500 cc class, in Germany, on the old Nürburgring circuit. Riding an MV he finishes ahead of a whole squad of two-stroke Suzukis) For MV it would the last ever victory.

1977 Wins his last Italian Championship title.

1977 On 25th September he achieves the last victory of his career on a Yamaha 750 (GP of Germany, Hockenheim).

1977 On 2nd October he takes place in his last motorbike race on the Mugello Circuit. Riding on a Yamaha 350, an engine problem causes him to crash on the final lap.

1977 At the age of 35 Agostini announces, on 22nd December, his retirement from motorcycle racing.

1978 Begins to race cars and takes part in the European Formula 2 Championship

1979 Participates in Formula Aurora, which used Formula 1 cars from the previous year's World Championship.

1980 Races for the last time in Formula 1 Aurora.

1982 Team Agostini makes its debut in the World Motorcycling Championship.

1984 Wins his first world title as Eddie Lawson's team manager (Yamaha 500). Goes on to take the 500 cc titles in 1986 and 1988, again with Lawson.

1988 On 18th June marries Maria Ayuso in Andalusia (Spain).

1989 Daughter Victoria born in 17th May.

1991 Becomes Manager of the Cagiva team in the 500 cc class. Signs Eddie Lawson for two seasons.

1992 Lawson takes the first GP win for Caviga in the 500 cc class (Hungarian GP).

1994 Son Piergiacomo born on 22nd November.

1994 Caviga withdraws from the World Championship at the end

Puerto de Santa Maria, Cadice, Spain, 1988: bride Maria becomes the first woman ever to be allowed to ride pillion.

Snaps from the wedding album. Above: the ceremony with the bride's father, José Luis (left), and the groom's mother, Maria Vittoria (right).
Below: Ago arrives at the church with his mother.

At the age of forty-five, following a daredevil career, Agostini meets the love of his life: Maria Ayuso.

Children shortly followed. First Vittoria, then Piergiacomo, known as “Giacomino”. Almost immediately, they became a common sight at World Championship races.

An MV revival at Cascina Costa, with Vittoria and Piergiacomo following father along. Giacomino gets ready to hand Ago his helmet.

Above: on rare occasions Ago still dons his leathers.
Below: presenting the MV Agusta F4, which he helped develop.

A special occasion: Maria and Giacomo Agostini present King Juan Carlos of Spain, a keen motorcycling enthusiast, with a brand new MV Agusta F4.

On 29th May 2003 Giacomo Agostini is made *Commendatore* of the Italian Republic by the Head of State, Carlo Azeglio Ciampi.

of the season after having won a total of three GPs in the 500 cc class. It is Agostini's last year as a motorcycling team manager.

1998 Agostini celebrates the return of the MV Agusta (now owned by the Castiglioni brothers, also owners of Caviga) and introduces the F4, a motorcycle he helped develop and promote.

2003 Nominated *Commendatore della Repubblica* by Head of State, Carlo Azeglio Ciampi

KEY: unclass. = unclassified (in championship); DNF = did not finish; DNQ = did not qualify; DNS = did not start race

Records and victories

RECORDS

Greatest ever number of World Championship titles: 15
The most victorious rider in the 350 cc class: 7 titles
The most victorious rider in the 500 cc class: 8 titles
World Championship titles in 350 cc: 1968, 1969, 1970, 1971, 1972, 1973 and 1974
World Championship titles in 500 cc: 1966, 1967, 1968, 1969, 1970, 1971, 1972 and 1975.

The only rider to have won the World Championship in two different classes (350 and 500 cc) in the same season fo five years running: 1968 -1969-1970-1971-1972.
Winner of world championship titles for ten years from 1966 to 1975

Greatest ever number of GP victories: 122
Greatest ever number of victories in the World Championship 350 cc class 54
Greatest ever number of victories in the World Championship 500 cc class 68
Greatest ever number of consecutive victories in the 500 cc 1968 / 1969 20
Victorious 40 times in two categories (350 and 500) in the same GP
58 consecutive victories in 350 and 500 cc Grand Prix races (1968 - 1971)
Greatest ever number of wins in a single season (equalling Hailwood's 1966 record): 1970 - 19 overall GP wins in both 350 and 500 cc)

Second greatest number of wins in a single season in 500 cc: 1972 - 11 GPs won (the record belongs to Michael Doohan - 1997 with 12 GP wins).
World championship Grand Prix wins in a single season:
19 in 1970 10 in 500 cc - 9 in 350 cc
18 in 1969 10 in 500 cc - 8 in 350 cc
17 in 1968 10 in 500 cc - 7 in 350 cc
17 in 1972 11 in 500 cc - 6 in 350 cc
Same-year winner in both the Daytona 200 and the Imola 200 (equalling Jarno Saarinen, 1973): 1974
Victories at the Isle of Man TT race: 10 (5 Senior 500 cc - 5 Junior 350 cc).

VICTORIES

Thirteen years of success in the World Championships

Year	Victories in G.P	Motorcycle
1965	4	MV Agusta
1966	6	MV Agusta
1967	6	MV Agusta
1968	17	MV Agusta
1969	18	MV Agusta
1970	19	MV Agusta
1971	14	MV Agusta
1972	17	MV Agusta
1973	7	MV Agusta
1974	7	Yamaha
1975	5	Yamaha
1976	2	MV Agusta
1977	1	Yamaha

Victories in the World Championship

Year	Motorcycle	350 cc GP	500 cc GP	750 cc GPs	World Titles	TT
1963	Morini	–	–	–	–	–
1964	Morini	–	–	–	–	–
1965	MV Agusta	3	1	–	–	–
1966	MV Agusta	3	3	–	500	350
1967	MV Agusta	1	5	–	500	–
1968	MV Agusta	10	7	–	350-500	350-500
1969	MV Agusta	8	10	–	350-500	350-500
1970	MV Agusta	9	10	–	350-500	350-500
1971	MV Agusta	6	8	–	350-500	500
1972	MV Agusta	6	11	–	350-500	350-500
1973	MV Agusta	4	3	–	350	–
1974	Yamaha	5	2	–	350	–
1975	Yamaha	1	4	–	500	–
1976	MV Agusta	1	1	–	–	–
1977	Yamaha	–	–	1	–	–
Total		54	68	1	15	10

World Championships ratings

Year	Rating	Class	Bike	GP races disputed
1963	unclass.	250 cc	Morini	1 out of 10
1964	10th	250 cc	Morini	2 out of 11
1965	2nd	350 cc	MV Agusta	8 out of 9
1965	2nd	500 cc	MV Agusta	8 out of 10
1966	2nd	350 cc	MV Agusta	9 out of 10
1966	1st	500 cc	MV Agusta	9 out of 9
1967	2nd	350 cc	MV Agusta	8 out of 8
1967	1st	500 cc	MV Agusta	10 out of 10
1968	1st	350 cc	MV Agusta	7 out of 7
1968	1st	500 cc	MV Agusta	10 out of 10
1969	1st	350 cc	MV Agusta	8 out of 10

1969	1st	500 cc	MV Agusta	10 out of 12
1970	1st	350 cc	MV Agusta	9 out of 10
1970	1st	500 cc	MV Agusta	10 out of 11
1971	1st	350 cc	MV Agusta	9 out of 11
1971	1st	500 cc	MV Agusta	9 out of 11
1972	1st	350 cc	MV Agusta	11 out of 12
1972	1st	500 cc	MV Agusta	12 out of 13
1973	1st	350 cc	MV Agusta	9 out of 11
1973	3rd	500 cc	MV Agusta	8 out of 11
1974	1st	350 cc	Yamaha	6 out of 10
1974	4th	500 cc	Yamaha	7 out of 10
1975	2nd	350 cc	Yamaha	8 out of 10
1975	1st	500 cc	Yamaha	9 out of 10
1976	15th	350 cc	MV Agusta Yamaha	8 out of 10
1976	7th	500 cc	MV Agusta Suzuki	9 out of 10
1977	18th	350 cc	Yamaha	10 out of 11
1977	6th	500 cc	Yamaha	9 out of 11
1977	3rd	750 cc	Yamaha	5 out of 11

GP results in the world championship

Year	Position	Class	Motorbike	Circuit	GP
1963	DNF	250 cc	Morini	Monza	Italy
1964	4th	250 cc	Morini	Solitude	Germany
1964	4th	250 cc	Morini	Monza	Italy
1965	1st	350 cc	MV Agusta	Nurburgring	Germany
1965	2nd	500 cc	MV Agusta	Nurburgring	Germany
1965	3rd	350 cc	MV Agusta	Isle of Man	TT Junior
1965	DNF	500 cc	MV Agusta	Isle of Man	TT Senior
1965	3rd	350 cc	MV Agusta	Assen	TT Holland
1965	2nd	500 cc	MV Agusta	Assen	TT Holland
1965	2nd	500 cc	MV Agusta	Spa-Francor	Belgium
1965	DNF	350 cc	MV Agusta	Sachsenring	East Germany
1965	2nd	500 cc	MV Agusta	Sachsenring	East Germany
1965	DNF	350 cc	MV Agusta	Brno	Czech
1965	2nd	500 cc	MV Agusta	Brno	Czech

1965	1st	350 cc	MV Agusta	Imatra	Finland
1965	1st	500 cc	MV Agusta	Imatra	Finland
1965	1st	350 cc	MV Agusta	Monza	Italy
1965	2nd	500 cc	MV Agusta	Monza	Italy
1965	5th	350 cc	MV Agusta	Suzuka	Japan
1966	DNF	350 cc	MV Agusta	Hockenheim	Germany
1966	2nd	500 cc	MV Agusta	Hockenheim	Germany
1966	2nd	350 cc	MV Agusta	Cl. Ferrand	France
1966	2nd	350 cc	MV Agusta	Assen	TT Holland
1966	2nd	500 cc	MV Agusta	Assen	TT Holland
1966	1st	500 cc	MV Agusta	Spa-Francor	Belgium
1966	1st	350 cc	MV Agusta	Sachsenring	East Germany
1966	DNF	500 cc	MV Agusta	Sachsenring	East Germany
1966	2nd	350 cc	MV Agusta	Brno	Czech
1966	2nd	500 cc	MV Agusta	Brno	Czech
1966	DNF	350 cc	MV Agusta	Imatra	Finland
1966	1st	500 cc	MV Agusta	Imatra	Finland
1966	2nd	350 cc	MV Agusta	Dundrod	Ireland
1966	2nd	500 cc	MV Agusta	Dundrod	Ireland
1966	1st	350 cc	MV Agusta	Isle of Man	TT Junior
1966	2nd	500 cc	MV Agusta	Isle of Man	TT Senior
1966	1st	350 cc	MV Agusta	Monza	Italy
1966	1st	500 cc	MV Agusta	Monza	Italy
1967	2nd	350 cc	MV Agusta	Hockenheim	Germany
1967	1st	500 cc	MV Agusta	Hockenheim	Germany
1967	2nd	350 cc	MV Agusta	Isle of Man	TT Junior
1967	DNF	500 cc	MV Agusta	Isle of Man	TT Senior
1967	2nd	350 cc	MV Agusta	Assen	Holland
1967	2nd	500 cc	MV Agusta	Assen	Holland
1967	1st	500 cc	MV Agusta	Spa-Francor	Belgium
1967	2nd	350 cc	MV Agusta	Sachsenring	East Germany
1967	1st	500 cc	MV Agusta	Sachsenring	East Germany
1967	7th	350 cc	MV Agusta	Brno	Czech
1967	2nd	500 cc	MV Agusta	Brno	Czech
1967	1st	500 cc	MV Agusta	Imatra	Finland
1967	1st	350 cc	MV Agusta	Dundrod	Ireland
1967	20th	500 cc	MV Agusta	Dundrod	Ireland
1967	DNF	350 cc	MV Agusta	Monza	Italy
1967	1st	500 cc	MV Agusta	Monza	Italy
1967	2nd	500 cc	MV Agusta	Mosport	Canada

1968	1st	350 cc	MV Agusta	Nurburgring	Germany
1968	1st	500 cc	MV Agusta	Nurburgring	Germany
1968	1st	500 cc	MV Agusta	Barcelona	Spain
1968	1st	350 cc	MV Agusta	Isle of Man	TT Junior
1968	1st	500 cc	MV Agusta	Isle of Man	TT Senior
1968	1st	350 cc	MV Agusta	Assen	Holland
1968	1st	500 cc	MV Agusta	Assen	Holland
1968	1st	500 cc	MV Agusta	Spa-Francor	Belgium
1968	1st	350 cc	MV Agusta	Sachsenring	East Germany
1968	1st	500 cc	MV Agusta	Sachsenring	East Germany
1968	1st	350 cc	MV Agusta	Brno	Czech
1968	1st	500 cc	MV Agusta	Brno	Czech
1968	1st	500 cc	MV Agusta	Imatra	Finland
1968	1st	350 cc	MV Agusta	Dundrod	Ireland
1968	1st	500 cc	MV Agusta	Dundrod	Ireland
1968	1st	350 cc	MV Agusta	Monza	Italy
1968	1st	500 cc	MV Agusta	Monza	Italy
1969	1st	350 cc	MV Agusta	Jarama	Spain
1969	1st	500 cc	MV Agusta	Jarama	Spain
1969	1st	350 cc	MV Agusta	Hockenheim	Germany
1969	1st	500 cc	MV Agusta	Hockenheim	Germany
1969	1st	500 cc	MV Agusta	Le Mans	France
1969	1st	350 cc	MV Agusta	Isle of Man	TT Junior
1969	1st	500 cc	MV Agusta	Isle of Man	TT Senior
1969	1st	350 cc	MV Agusta	Assen	TT Holland
1969	1st	500 cc	MV Agusta	Assen	TT Holland
1969	1st	500 cc	MV Agusta	Spa-Francor	Belgium
1969	1st	350 cc	MV Agusta	Sachsenring	East Germany
1969	1st	500 cc	MV Agusta	Sachsenring	East Germany
1969	1st	350 cc	MV Agusta	Brno	Czech
1969	1st	500 cc	MV Agusta	Brno	Czech
1969	1st	350 cc	MV Agusta	Imatra	Finland
1969	1st	500 cc	MV Agusta	Imatra	Finland
1969	1st	350 cc	MV Agusta	Dundrod	Ireland
1969	1st	500 cc	MV Agusta	Dundrod	Ireland
1970	1st	350 cc	MV Agusta	Nurburgring	Germany
1970	1st	500 cc	MV Agusta	Nurburgring	Germany
1970	1st	500 cc	MV Agusta	Le Mans	France
1970	1st	350 cc	MV Agusta	Opatija	Yugoslavia
1970	1st	500 cc	MV Agusta	Opatija	Yugoslavia

1970	1st	350 cc	MV Agusta	Isle of Man	TT Junior
1970	1st	500 cc	MV Agusta	Isle of Man	TT Senior
1970	1st	350 cc	MV Agusta	Assen	TT Holland
1970	1st	500 cc	MV Agusta	Assen	TT Holland
1970	1st	500 cc	MV Agusta	Spa-Francor	Belgium
1970	1st	350 cc	MV Agusta	Sachsenring	East Germany
1970	1st	500 cc	MV Agusta	Sachsenring	East Germany
1970	1st	350 cc	MV Agusta	Brno	Czech
1970	1st	350 cc	MV Agusta	Imatra	Finland
1970	1st	500 cc	MV Agusta	Imatra	Finland
1970	1st	350 cc	MV Agusta	Dundrod	Ireland
1970	1st	500 cc	MV Agusta	Dundrod	Ireland
1970	1st	350 cc	MV Agusta	Monza	Italy
1970	1st	500 cc	MV Agusta	Monza	Italy
1971	1st	350 cc	MV Agusta	Salzburg	Austria
1971	1st	500 cc	MV Agusta	Salzburg	Austria
1971	1st	350 cc	MV Agusta	Hockenheim	Germany
1971	1st	500 cc	MV Agusta	Hockenheim	Germany
1971	DNF	350 cc	MV Agusta	Isle of Man	TT Junior
1971	1st	500 cc	MV Agusta	Isle of Man	TT Senior
1971	1st	350 cc	MV Agusta	Assen	Holland
1971	1st	500 cc	MV Agusta	Assen	Holland
1971	1st	500 cc	MV Agusta	Spa-Francor	Belgium
1971	1st	350 cc	MV Agusta	Sachsenring	East Germany
1971	1st	500 cc	MV Agusta	Sachsenring	East Germany
1971	DNF	350 cc	MV Agusta	Brno	Czech
1971	1st	350 cc	MV Agusta	Anderstorp	Sweden
1971	1st	500 cc	MV Agusta	Anderstorp	Sweden
1971	1st	350 cc	MV Agusta	Imatra	Finland
1971	1st	500 cc	MV Agusta	Imatra	Finland
1971	DNF	350 cc	MV Agusta	Monza	Italy
1971	DNF	500 cc	MV Agusta	Monza	Italy
1972	2nd	350 cc	MV Agusta	Nurburgring	Germany
1972	1st	500 cc	MV Agusta	Nurburgring	Germany
1972	4th	350 cc	MV Agusta	C. Ferrand	France
1972	1st	500 cc	MV Agusta	C. Ferrand	France
1972	1st	350 cc	MV Agusta	Salzburg	Austria
1972	1st	500 cc	MV Agusta	Salzburg	Austria
1972	1st	350 cc	MV Agusta	Imola	Italy
1972	1st	500 cc	MV Agusta	Imola	Italy

1972	1st	350 cc	MV Agusta	Isle of Man	TT Junior
1972	1st	500 cc	MV Agusta	Isle of Man	TT Senior
1972	DNF	350 cc	MV Agusta	Opatija	Yugoslavia
1972	DNF	500 cc	MV Agusta	Opatija	Yugoslavia
1972	1st	350 cc	MV Agusta	Assen	TT Holland
1972	1st	500 cc	MV Agusta	Assen	TT Holland
1972	1st	500 cc	MV Agusta	Spa-Francor	Belgium
1972	DNF	350 cc	MV Agusta	Sachsenring	East Germany
1972	1st	500 cc	MV Agusta	Sachsenring	East Germany
1972	DNF	350 cc	MV Agusta	Brno	Czech
1972	1st	500 cc	MV Agusta	Brno	Czech
1972	1st	350 cc	MV Agusta	Anderstorp	Sweden
1972	1st	500 cc	MV Agusta	Anderstorp	Sweden
1972	1st	350 cc	MV Agusta	Imatra	Finland
1972	1st	500 cc	MV Agusta	Imatra	Finland
1973	1st	350 cc	MV Agusta	P. Ricard	France
1973	DNF	500 cc	MV Agusta	P. Ricard	France
1973	DNF	350 cc	MV Agusta	Salzburg	Austria
1973	DNF	500 cc	MV Agusta	Salzburg	Austria
1973	DNF	350 cc	MV Agusta	Hockenheim	Germany
1973	DNF	500 cc	MV Agusta	Hockenheim	Germany
1973	1st	350 cc	MV Agusta	Monza	Italy
1973	1st	350 cc	MV Agusta	Assen	TT Holland
1973	DNF	500 cc	MV Agusta	Assen	TT Holland
1973	1st	500 cc	MV Agusta	Spa-Francor	Belgium
1973	2nd	350 cc	MV Agusta	Brno	Czech
1973	1st	500 cc	MV Agusta	Brno	Czech
1973	2nd	350 cc	MV Agusta	Anderstorp	Sweden
1973	2nd	500 cc	MV Agusta	Anderstorp	Sweden
1973	1st	350 cc	MV Agusta	Imatra	Finland
1973	1st	500 cc	MV Agusta	Imatra	Finland
1974	1st	350 cc	Yamaha	C. Ferrand	France
1974	DNF	500 cc	Yamaha	C. Ferrand	France
1974	1st	350 cc	Yamaha	Salzburg	Austria
1974	1st	500 cc	Yamaha	Salzburg	Austria
1974	1st	350 cc	Yamaha	Imola	Italy
1974	DNF	500 cc	Yamaha	Imola	Italy
1974	1st	350 cc	Yamaha	Assen	TT Holland
1974	1st	500 cc	Yamaha	Assen	TT Holland
1974	2nd	500 cc	Yamaha	Spa-Francor	Belgium

1974	DNS	350 cc	Yamaha	Anderstorp	Sweden
1974	DNF	500 cc	Yamaha	Anderstorp	Sweden
1974	6th	500 cc	Yamaha	Brno	Czech
1974	1st	350 cc	Yamaha	Opatija	Yugoslavia
1975	2nd	350 cc	Yamaha	Le Castellet	France
1975	1st	500 cc	Yamaha	Le Castellet	France
1975	1st	350 cc	Yamaha	Jarama	Spain
1975	DNF	350 cc	Yamaha	Salzburg	Austria
1975	DNF	500 cc	Yamaha	Salzburg	Austria
1975	DNF	350 cc	Yamaha	Hockenheim	Germany
1975	1st	500 cc	Yamaha	Hockenheim	Germany
1975	2nd	350 cc	Yamaha	Imola	Italy
1975	1st	500 cc	Yamaha	Imola	Italy
1975	4th	350 cc	Yamaha	Assen	TT Holland
1975	2nd	500 cc	Yamaha	Assen	TT Holland
1975	DNF	500 cc	Yamaha	Spa-Francor	Belgium
1975	DNF	500 cc	Yamaha	Anderstorp	Sweden
1975	2nd	350 cc	Yamaha	Imatra	Finland
1975	1st	500 cc	Yamaha	Imatra	Finland
1975	DNF	350 cc	Yamaha	Brno	Czech
1975	2nd	500 cc	Yamaha	Brno	Czech
1976	DNF	350 cc	MV Agusta	Le Mans	France
1976	5th	500 cc	MV Agusta	Le Mans	France
1976	DNF	350 cc	MV Agusta	Salzburg	Austria
1976	6th	500 cc	MV Agusta	Salzburg	Austria
1976	DNF	350 cc	MV Agusta	Mugello	Italy
1976	DNF	500 cc	Suzuki	Mugello	Italy
1976	DNF	350 cc	MV Agusta	Opatija	Yugoslavia
1976	1st	350 cc	MV Agusta	Assen	TT Holland
1976	DNF	500 cc	Suzuki	Assen	TT Holland
1976	DNF	500 cc	Suzuki	Spa-Francor	Belgium
1976	DNF	350 cc	MV Agusta	Imatra	Finland
1976	DNF	500 cc	Suzuki	Imatra	Finland
1976	DNF	350 cc	MV Agusta	Brno	Czech
1976	DNF	500 cc	Suzuki	Brno	Czech
1976	DNF	350 cc	MV Agusta	Nurburgring	Germany
1976	1st	500 cc	MV Agusta	Nurburgring	Germany
1977	5th	500 cc	Yamaha	Imola	Italy
1977	2nd	500 cc	Yamaha	Le Castellet	France
1977	DNF	500 cc	Yamaha	Assen	TT Holland

1977	8th	500 cc	Yamaha	Spa-Francor	Belgium
1977	9th	500 cc	Yamaha	Anderstorp	Sweden
1977	DNF	500 cc	Yamaha	Imatra	Finland
1977	2nd	500 cc	Yamaha	Brno	Czech
1977	9th	500 cc	Yamaha	Silverstone	Great Britain
1977	3rd	750 cc	Yamaha	Imola	Italy
1977	2nd	750 cc	Yamaha	Salzburg	Austria
1977	4th	750 cc	Yamaha	Assen	TT Holland
1977	1st	750 cc	Yamaha	Hockenheim	Germany

European Formula 2

Year	Circuit	Car	Qual. result	Race result
1978	Thruxton	Chevron B42	–	18th
1978	Hockenheim	Chevron B42	DNQ	–
1978	Nurburgring	Chevron B42	–	18th
1978	Pau	Chevron B42	DNF	–
1978	Mugello	Chevron B42	–	17th
1978	Vallelunga	Chevron B42	DNQ	–
1978	Rouen	Chevron B42	DNQ	–
1978	Donington Park	Chevron B42	DNQ	–
1978	Nogaro	Chevron B42	DNQ	–
1978	Pergusa	Chevron B42	DNQ	–
1978	Misano adriatico	Chevron B42	DNQ	–
1978	Hockenheim	March 782	–	16th

Formula 1 Aurora

Year	Circuit	Car	Qual. result	Race result
1979	Zolder	Williams FW06-1	5	9th
1979	Oulton Park	Williams FW06-1	8	6th
1979	Brands Hatch	Williams FW06-1	11	DNF
1979	Snetterton	Williams FW06-2	4	2nd
1979	Thruxton	Williams FW06-2	13	6th
1979	Zandvoort	Williams FW06-1	8	3rd
1979	Donington	Williams FW06-1	5	9th

1979	Oulton Park	Williams FW06-1	8	3rd
1979	Nogaro	Williams FW06-1	17	DNF
1979	Mallory Park	Williams FW06-1	5	DNF
1979	Brands-Hatch	Williams FW06-1	9	DNF
1979	Thruxton	Williams FW06-1	10	6th
1979	Snetterton	Williams FW06-1	10	7th
1979	Silverstone	Williams FW06-1	10	7th
1980	Brands Hatch	Williams FW06-5	7	4th
1980	Silverstone	Williams FW06-5	5	DNF
1980	Thruxton	Williams FW06-2	5	4th
1980	Monza	Williams FW06-2	2	3rd
1980	Snetterton	Williams FW06-2	4	DNF
1980	Brands Hatch	Williams FW06-2	7	3rd
1980	Thruxton	Williams FW06-2	3	3rd
1980	Silverstone	Williams FW06-2	3	3rd

Printed May 2006
for Fucina Srl
by GSA of S. Angelo Lodigiano (Lodi, Italy)

